The Story-Time of the British Empire

The Story-Time of the British Empire

Colonial and Postcolonial Folkloristics

SADHANA NAITHANI

UNIVERSITY PRESS OF MISSISSIPPI • JACKSON

www.upress.state.ms.us

The University Press of Mississippi is a member of
the Association of American University Presses.

Copyright © 2010 by University Press of Mississippi
All rights reserved
Manufactured in the United States of America

First printing 2010

∞

Library of Congress Cataloging-in-Publication Data

Naithani, Sadhana.
The story-time of the British empire : colonial and postcolonial folkloristics / Sadhana Naithani.
  p. cm.
Includes bibliographical references and index.
ISBN 978-1-60473-455-3 (cloth : alk. paper) — ISBN 978-1-60473-456-0 (ebook)
1. Tales. 2. Folklore. 3. Folklorists. 4. Great Britain—Colonies. I. Title.
GR305.N265 2010
398.20941—dc22   2010001902

British Library Cataloging-in-Publication Data available

*In loving memory of my Grandfather
Sri Ram Naithani,
whose pocket watch from the days of the Empire
still clocks time, in my laptop bag.*

CONTENTS

Preface (IX)

Acknowledgments (XI)

CHAPTER 1.
Fields: Colonialism, Folklore, and Postcolonial Theory
(1)

CHAPTER 2.
Motive: The Contexts of Colonial Folklorists
(11)

CHAPTER 3.
Method: The Striving of Colonial Folklorists
(23)

CHAPTER 4.
Theory: Colonial Theories of Folklore
(76)

CHAPTER 5.
The Story-Time of the British Empire:
Transnational Folkloristics as Theory of Cultural Disjunctions
(115)

Notes (129)

References (135)

Index (140)

PREFACE

The importance of storytelling in the personal and public lives of individuals and societies cannot be overstated. We know that entertainment is only one of its purposes, and there are other more important purposes associated with it, like education, projection of self or of group, representation of others, documentation, and narration of history. Cultures are formed, reformed, and destroyed in the process of storytelling. Political powers, too, are accompanied by storytelling in the process of their establishment and assertion. The role of Hollywood movies in the expansion of American influence world-wide cannot be overstated, nor that of Bollywood in the making of India's postcolonial identity. However, both of these are phenomena of the twentieth century, and neither belongs to an Empire like the British Empire in the late nineteenth and early twentieth centuries—an Empire without which the United States and India would not have been what they are today, nor would the rest of the world have been what it is. The postcolonial world is the world after the British Empire. How did this Empire create its identity? How did it communicate its identity? What stories did it tell about itself? How did it create those stories? What do those stories have to do with our perception of the world today?

The popularity of evening or night as the time for telling stories across the world is well known, but *the sun did not set on the British Empire*—proverbially speaking. So what was the story-time of the British Empire? This is a book about that phase of the Empire when it started telling stories about itself to its own people and to others about its peoples.

ACKNOWLEDGMENTS

The research for this book was done over a long period of time and largely with personal funding. Therefore, support at the personal level remained crucial to its completion and deserves the first acknowledgments. I am thankful to my husband Sudheer Gupta for his creative and radical financial advice, which made the international logistics of this research fathomable. I thank my parents for the energy their encouragement has provided me. Research for this work was done in London during various stays. I thank Judith and Philip Woods for hosting me affectionately and showing me London from their insiders' perspective.

The vastness and the volume of materials required to be studied for this research would have been daunting, but for the resources of the Folklore Society, London. I thank Dr. Caroline Oates, Assistant Librarian, for her invaluable cooperation in the process of my scanning the FLS collections.

I thank Jawaharlal Nehru University for the Study Leave granted to me in 2004–2005 during which I wrote the first draft of this book. A research grant from the Charles Wallace Trust of the British Council made it possible for me to check the entire materials and other sources in London before finalizing this manuscript in May–June 2008. For this, I thank Richard Alford, Director of the Charles Wallace Trust.

I am grateful to friends and colleagues who have regularly heard my thoughts as they emerged and responded on them: the careful reading of my manuscript by Margaret Mills is responsible for the finer final version; Cristina Bacchilega and Diarmuid Ó Giolláin enlightened me with their own concerns with colonialism and folklore; Charles Briggs invited me to teach for a semester at the University of California, Berkeley, in 2007 and in dialogue with him I learned to think of colonialism in wider contexts than that of the British Empire; Graham Furniss and John Parker of the School of Oriental and African Studies, London, discussed with me the African side of this research and I am very thankful for their engagement.

This work could not be conceptualized without redefining disciplinary boundaries and accepting the task of checking and counter-checking my own perspectives and methods. I have taken every care to do so and am responsible for whatever I might have overlooked or misunderstood.

The Story-Time of the British Empire

CHAPTER I

Fields

Colonialism, Folklore, and Postcolonial Theory

In folklore studies throughout the twentieth century, scholars have studied their materials within the boundaries of modern nation states. Therefore, barring comparative analyses between folklore of one country or community and that of another country or community, the history of folklore research, critical studies on folklore collectors and their ideologies, and the socio-political implications of folklore studies have all been seen within national boundaries. This is probably natural for a discipline whose emergence is understood in folklore theory as rooted in the context of the building of modern nation states in Europe.[1] From the concept to its practice, "collection of folklore" is understood to have started as an engagement of middle-class intellectuals, poets, and writers with the narratives and songs that were common among the majority populace of a society, namely Germany, in transition from feudal to modern systems, and from small principalities to a nation. The history of folklore as a subject and object of research is traced back to the early nineteenth-century romantic-nationalist movement in Germany, to the works of the Grimm brothers and to their international influence (Ó Giolláin 2000, 44). However, this feature of folklore studies is based not only in historical context(s) of the discipline, but also in the perspective of the discipline itself.

The global history of folklore research is Eurocentric in its approach to the extent that it is based on nineteenth-century European folklore collectors *within* Europe, although it is well known that in the same century a large number of Europeans collected folklore of countries on other continents. Much of this work outside the European continent was accomplished in the context of colonial relations and done by non-folklorists, yet oral narrative and poetic expressions of peoples of other continents were collected, transcribed, translated, published, and discussed internationally. Folklore studies have not taken into consideration a major phase in the history of the discipline: folklore collection and scholarship in the colonial Empires, including the British Empire.

Debates in literary, historical, and cultural studies since the 1970s have shown that colonial hegemonic systems created, and were created by, intellectual paradigms. Edward Said called this "Orientalism" (1977). Mary Louise Pratt called it "The Imperial Gaze" (1992). Many other theoretical positions have been identified with the term "post-colonial theory." In Foucault's terminology we could say that colonialism created its own "archaeology of knowledge." The commonality in these different streams of thought is that they examine the processes in which knowledge about societies and peoples has been generated, constructed, and disseminated, and which in turn contributed to the existence, furtherance, and establishment of political and ideological colonial hegemonies. To put it differently, theories in the humanities have since the 1970s stressed that colonial hegemony is not only about establishment of political systems, but also about its acute implications in the cross-cultural perceptions of peoples and societies. From savage, to noble savage, to primitive, to backward civilizations, to developing countries, it has been the growth of a certain idea, in which the colonized were the savage, the primitive, and the backward. In their more recent histories—that is, since gaining independence from colonial rule—they were the under-developed, and then the developing societies. Though they had gained independence, yet cultural notions and ideological perceptions about their people continued to be based in the archaeology of knowledge constructed in the eighteenth and nineteenth centuries. In the academia this archeology has been actively deconstructed in the second half of the twentieth century by theories that have been identified as postcolonial—both in terms of historical chronology and ideological bent. One could say that the common element in the wide variety of research subjects studied with postcolonial perspectives is a critical questioning of colonial paradigms. New streams of thoughts have emerged from the glaciers of the independence movements within the colonies in the first half of the twentieth century. These steams have been further nurtured by the growth of new intellectual environments after these countries became independent. Postcolonial theory has emerged from different parts of the world, yet its concerns have been defined by national boundaries, and not by the international boundaries of the colonial Empire.

Where does oral discourse figure in all this? Most of the above mentioned theories are based either in literature or history. Oral discourse seems to be nowhere. The discipline of which folklore collection[2] was a part, anthropology, has also had a postcolonial engagement with its colonial past. Since the 1960s, anthropologists have critiqued and analyzed colonial anthropology as largely subservient to the colonial power structures.[3] Colonial folklore collectors have not figured in this in a major way. Although folklore was often only a part of big anthropological projects, yet it was a part with a distinct identity, always bordering on an independent existence. "Folklore" thus formed one or more independent chapters in an anthropological work. These chapters could be accessed directly for information and entertainment. It is understandable that critical perspectives in anthropology did not engage with colonial folklore collectors, but it is not equally understandable as to why the critical perspectives of the 1960s did not motivate folklorists to review colonial folklore collections. This applies to folklorists within the erstwhile colonized and the colonizing countries, and in other locations, like the United States, where much of postcolonial theory emerged. Folklorists apparently remained oblivious to new theoretical paradigms. For instance, almost at the beginning of the change in perspectives, William Bascom's article "Folklore Research in Africa" is a discussion on the available materials—a bibliography. At one level, he is "surprised" (Bascom 1964, 12) that there is so much material on African folklore, and at another level, he does not seem to notice the connection between most of the works listed in his bibliography and colonialism, or that many of these folklore collectors were colonial administrators and other representatives of colonizing nations. Even analytical works on the history of British folklore studies do not include the British collectors who compiled collections in the colonies. History of British folkloristics is based on the folklore compilations within England. This is an artificial boundary, particularly for the nineteenth and twentieth centuries, considering that the colonial folklore collectors' intended audiences were always in England, and considering the role the Folk-Lore Society, London, played in the growth of the transnational endeavors. It was home to British folklore collectors and collections from all over the Empire, and the colonial collectors certainly outnumbered those based in England. Their collections occupied the center stage of scholarly debates for decades and opened windows to new worlds for the general readers. But since the termination of the imperial rule in the middle of the twentieth century, British folkloristics has all but formally forgotten the colonial collectors from its history.

The colonial archaeology of knowledge was organized under different disciplinary heads, but was based in the oral sources. This applies to all erstwhile colonized countries and as such "orality" has relevance to all scholars of colonialism. The history of colonial folklore scholarship is thus central to understanding culture theory and culture politics of colonialism. Colonialists' collections of folklore of many different formerly colonized peoples remain the first and only record of their late nineteenth-century folklore. "Nationalist" scholarship of folklore in the colonies by the natives, if any, emerged only later, and is often neither as voluminous nor as expansive for the said period as that done by the colonizers. For this reason, academic courses, analytical works, and popular publications and perceptions are based on the colonial collections. They continue to represent and define the "culture" of these regions on both sides of the erstwhile colonial divide.[4] An irony embedded in the standard discourse escapes us: that the history of folkloristics in the United Kingdom can be written without reference to its colonial past, but the history of folkloristics in erstwhile colonized countries must begin in the colonial past. This "irony" slips in the question: do the colonial collections of folklore from different colonies belong (in the sense of an intellectual tradition) to those individual colonies such as India, or to the British? One could extend the field of inquiry and ask: are the histories of folkloristics in India connected with those in Africa or Australia, considering that they were part of the same Empire and their folklores were translated into the English language and collected by individuals who met with each other in the Folk-Lore Society, London? Indeed, as intellectual tradition the collected materials belong both to the individual countries concerned and to the British folkloristics. The second question—whether there are theoretical and methodological connections between colonial folklore collection of Asia, Africa, and Australia—will be answered in the affirmative by the present study. On the grounds of these connections, among other crucial features, I will argue that "colonial folkloristics" should be accepted as the term that takes the transnational identity of the phenomena into consideration, and can be applicable across the epistemic and empirical boundaries between the colonizer and the colonized.

Colonial folkloristics can only be studied and analyzed beyond national boundaries, because it was not created within a nation. It was also not created between two countries, but in a global context. Above all, it was also not created by individuals of any one culture alone. Contrary to the standard genealogies, the voluminous colonial folklore collections were not created by British collectors alone. In asserting this point I am *not* referring to the well-known and faceless image of a "native assistant," but to the conscious involvement of Africans and Asians in the making of these collections. Their role remained largely obscured until the emergence of the English manuscripts of north Indian folktales in the handwriting of an Indian (Naithani 2002a, 2002b, 2006a). The present study will show that individuals of varying capacities across the Empire associated with British collectors in extremely significant ways. The point is that the bipolar frame of colonizer and colonized is not sufficient for the analysis of colonial folkloristics.

In Great Britain, the Empire was the locale for folklore collection and identity building—a space not within the nation, but outside it. Nation is an "Imagined Community" (Anderson 1991), but what was the identity of an Empire that "was a grab-bag of primarily tropical possessions scattered over every continent" (ibid., 92)? Nation is at least "imagined" in the sense of "desired" by many, but the Empire was a statement of power and purpose of the nation. "Empire" existed, but no one knew it all, no one could have seen it all, nor could anyone have reached everywhere. The movement of people was largely in one direction, from metropole to the colonies, and "Only a minority of the subjected peoples had any long-standing religious, linguistic, cultural, or even political and economic ties with the metropole" (ibid., 92). Yet, the fact of an Empire spread across many continents generated in the public sphere of the colonizing nation the desire to "know" and "tell" about the Empire and its inhabitants, and in colonies it generated the need to administrate and control people.

The identity of the Empire lay in the knowledge about the Empire and in the articulation of this knowledge. While many areas of this knowledge were of interest to only certain sections of the populace in the colonizing nation, some areas of knowledge were of interest to almost all sections of people. "Knowledge about natives" constituted a subject which was of general and scholarly interest. The whole Empire could be made into a comprehensible entity for the common people only by sketching out its various parts. The idea of Empire could hold even greater disparities and diversities than exist within a nation. And it functioned in this complex, semi-articulated fashion for a long period and shaped more than the economic and political future of the "center" and the "peripheries." In the following I would not use the terms periphery, because it confuses the virtual map of folkloristics that we have here.

However, generating knowledge about the Empire was not a simple task, because it had to be based on the knowledge of the "natives." In this process folklore played an important role because most colonies were predominantly oral cultures. Orality became the source of all kinds of writings on the colonized, but I argue that oral expression is most crystallized in folklore, because narratives and songs constitute spheres of highly structured orality. These particular forms of orality are most easily textualized, so they can become objects of remote contemplation. Later, photography and cinema provide a comparable ease for textualization of dance and other performative aspects of folklore, and museums for textualization of materials culture. In the global network of the British Empire, the relationship of each colony to the United Kingdom was clear, but the relationship of one colony with others was of different varieties. The venues where all the different units could be placed together were in England: from huge ministries to academic institutions and museums, from policies to analyses, from fossils to flora and fauna—all could be dealt with within common buildings by similar policies and theories. Specifically for folklore studies, the Folk-Lore Society, London, represented one such singular point: where folklore from the whole Empire could be put on the same table and discussed.

The Story-Time of the British Empire is an analytical study of not only what was placed on that table and sold in the markets, but also how and why it came to be placed on that table and sold in that market. This is a study of the processes of folklore collection in and dissemination from the British Empire. The subjects of analysis are the British writings on the "folklore" of different colonies compiled between 1850 and 1930.

As stated in the preface, the focus of this study is on South Asia and Africa in the British Empire. Collections of Australian folklore require special attention, because the process of colonizing Australia was so essentially different that collection of folklore there had an altogether different meaning. The general massacre of the aboriginal population lends a certain tragic irony to the "collections of folklore" or anthropological studies compiled from the survivors in rehabilitation camps and the like. The realization and articulation of this tragedy were expressed in colonial writings and folklore collections. Consider the case of Tasmania: "The island was discovered in 1642; the first small European settlement was established in 1803; and in 1877 (only seventy four years after this initial attempt at colonizing the island) the last surviving Tasmanian died. This record speaks for itself" (Balfour 1923, 14). The few works on Australian folklore that were compiled and published will remain in constant reference within this study. They present certain extremes of colonial folkloristics and highlight the fact that while speaking of colonial folkloristics we are dealing with its pluralities. The whole field cannot be defined by any one zone alone (for example, India), because each of its segments differs from others.

Folklore collections from English "colonies"—Ireland, Scotland, and Wales—are not included in this analysis, because of the very different nature of their colonization, especially at this stage of the British Empire—in the late nineteenth century. Ireland, Scotland, and Wales had been at one level part of the colonizing forces in Asia, Africa, and elsewhere; and at another level, they were going through nationalist movements within. Folklore scholarship in Ireland in the late nineteenth century was being led by nationalist forces (Ó Giolláin 2000, 94–113), and is therefore comparable with its European contemporaries, and not with Asian and African.[5] In the larger context of the British global cultural network, Ireland, Scotland, and Wales are the initial points of the intercontinental transfer of meanings.

British colonialism created a global cultural network that linked one with the "other" and "others" in synthetic ways and is at the crux of current hybrid cultures. While acknowledging the importance of Edward Said's "Orientalism" (1977) in the development of postcolonial theory, my study has a different route: it does not see the colonial world as bipolar—divided between binary categories of colonizer-colonized, self-other, and/or representer-represented. Instead, it proposes that colonialism be seen as a multinodal trail—beginning from a particular location and then going on to predictable and unpredictable terrains. In the process of this movement loops of cultural definitions emerge and each unit is linked to the other. In modern colonization, transformed oral expressive culture of different peoples into English language texts is a loop that ran across many regions, languages, and readers. Collection, translation, and publication of folklore gained unprecedented dimensions and brought the discipline of folkloristics onto a new plane.

First of all, colonial folkloristics challenges the idea of nation as the field of folkloristics. Colonialism generated a phase in folklore scholarship which transcended national boundaries at the level of collection and dissemination of the materials. Folklore collected in different colonies was published in Britain, and from there it traveled in many directions. Colonial folklore scholarship was *transnational* from the initial to the final stage. This I consider its defining characteristic, without the appreciation of which colonial folkloristics cannot be understood.

Second, British colonial folkloristics questions the standard assumption in folkloristics that "nationalism" was the sole socio-political context of nineteenth-century folkloristics. The British collectors of folklore in different colonies saw their nation also as the Empire, and the Empire was not only a bigger entity, but also another identity. The "subjects" of this transnational Empire were at least divided into two categories—the British and the non-

British. The contradiction and confrontation between the two was the quintessential reality of this Empire. And if class can be taken as the basic category within the nation to define the social hierarchies and contested power, then the Empire as conglomeration of different "nations" had the additional transnational hierarchy between the British and the non-British. This complexity is visible in the definition of folklore that most colonial collectors considered acceptable: "[Folklore] has established itself as the generic term under which the traditional Beliefs, Customs, Stories, Songs and sayings current among *backward peoples,* or retained by the *uncultured classes of more advanced peoples,* are comprehended and included" (Burne 1914, 1, emphasis added). Burne's definition supports the argument that colonial scholarship was not only a system of representing "other" peoples, but also the lower classes within Britain by clubbing "backward peoples" and "uncultured classes of more advanced peoples." This complexity is intrinsic to the structure of British folkloristics. Within the context of European nations, folklore became the symbol of national unity, but in the context of the British colonial Empire the processes were split: collection of folklore of the colonized was aimed at their better control, while the folklore collection at home had a rather diffused agenda.

Third, this phase of folklore scholarship presents a transformation of orality into written word, which is simultaneously multilingual and intercultural, because foreigners (British colonials) executed the transformation from many "native" languages (of colonized countries) into a "foreign" (English) language.

Fourth, in European nations mainly poets, writers, teachers, and other educated people compiled folklore. In the colonial contexts this role was performed by administrators, missionaries, and amateurs. Presumably and evidently, they brought different sensibilities to their work. Their expression was subsequently governed by dissimilar aims. Within Europe folklore was seen as one of the forms of cultural expressions. The images of the colonies of the British colonial Empire were constructed on oral discourse—in Asia, Africa, and Australia. Referring to the plurality of sources that make these images, African philosopher V. Y. Mudimbe says, "The discourses with which I am dealing belong to this colonial library created by the colonizer, the anthropologist and the missionary" (Mudimbe 1991, 4). These three—colonizer, anthropologist, and missionary—were different kinds of creators of data. The standard practice in folklore theory has been to evaluate the colonial folklore collectors dissociated from their official positions in the colonies. This does not seem justified to me, and for analytical purposes I will take both their positions into consideration wherever necessary.

COLONIAL FOLKLORE COLLECTIONS

The colonial writings on folklore exist in a few different forms, and some clarification is required as to the kind of writings on which this analysis is based. First of all, the works identified as "collections of folklore" (that is, folktales, songs, legends, and proverbs) by the compilers or collectors are under consideration. "Collections of folklore" are of different kinds, especially differing from each other on the scale of "scientific" methods: some were intended as popular books, for "general readers," others were meant for nurseries, and yet others were intended as "scientific" collections based on consciously decided methods and aims of collection. Often, the compilers of "scientific" volumes also produced the same materials in another form for larger readership—or their colleagues did, based on the original scientific works. (Rouse's *The Talking Thrush*, 1899, was meant for children and based on William Crooke's collection.) All these are under analytical consideration here.

Second, chapters on "folklore" in anthropological works are also treated at par with free-standing collections of folklore. Other chapters from the same volumes also reflect on the more specific engagement with folklore, and as such also influence analysis here.

Third, colonial writings on "customs and beliefs" of the colonized constitute clearly anthropological enquiries and as such are outside the scope of this work, but when customs and beliefs are expressed in tales or songs they enter the folkloristic margin, and their anthropological analysis comes close to folklore theory. Such "anthropological" works will be treated as part of colonial folkloristics. The working definition of "folklore" here is going to be text/genre based, because that was the operative definition for folkloristics in the late nineteenth and early twentieth centuries.

In the few available histories of colonial folklore collections (Dorson 1968; Jason 1983) three types of folklore collectors who mapped the terrain of folklore across the Empire have been identified: women, officials, and male missionaries. Quite obviously, the three categories refer to the primary role and gender identity of the collectors in the colonies where they collected folklore and not to their role as folklore collectors. Indeed, it is hard to find a "free" collector, that is, someone who had only gone to collect folklore, whether for scholarly or any other purpose. The three identified categories have been seen as three ways of coming to the idea of folklore collection. As regards methods and perspectives, within these three categories were individuals whose works differ from each other in many significant ways. Individuals from each category produced scholarly and popular collections, and held opinions that reflected many shades of colonial perceptions. I find this a simplistic categorization. The folklore of the "natives" and the collectors' identity interacted with each other in far more complex manners than are evident in these categories to determine the formats and contents of colonial folklore collections and scholarship.

I will therefore move away from this categorization of colonial folklore collectors as "missionaries-officers-women," and instead will discuss the colonial folklore scholarship with reference to primary categories of the science of folkloristics:

- *motives* that triggered the folklore collections in the minds of people whose main occupation in life was something else;
- *methods* adopted in the colonial context which became the bases of folklore theories; and
- *theory* in the colonial folklore collections.[6]

The three concepts—motives, methods, and theory—enclose among them the entire process of the transformation of orality into writing anywhere and at any point of time in the history of the discipline of folkloristics. By studying colonial folkloristics with reference to these three categories, it is intended that it be seen through universal terms of reference for the discipline of folkloristics—not ethnology, anthropology, or history, fields of study with which folkloristics is intimately related. Folkloristics has developed its own disciplinary system of analytical methods and categories. Colonial folklore collections and collectors have continued to be seen with ethnological and anthropological references. If one wishes to argue, as I do, that colonial folklore collections present a particular model of folklore research that needs to be identified and studied, then it is imperative that we identify it with reference to the contemporary terms of discourse in the discipline of folkloristics. Hence, although collectors' gender and other identities will be factors in my analysis, the primary components of the structure of this study will be *motive*, *method*, and *theory*, explored in the next three chapters, respectively. The concluding chapter will lay out the model of colonial folkloristics in terms of its parameters, its intellectual tradition, and its consequences for contemporary folklore studies.

CHAPTER 2

Motive

The Contexts of Colonial Folklorists

Folklorists present narrative and poetic texts born out of someone else's imagination. Their role in it is of a dilemmatic nature—as writers of the text they invariably mix their own words with those of the oral narrator, as translators they create unprecedented texts. Yet, they are not the tellers of these stories, but the "collectors" of these texts. The act of collection is not a natural creative urge, but a conscious decision based on a reason that "motivates" the author to initiate the act of collection. "Collection" is an intellectual activity in terms of its difference from creative expression. Collection requires systematization and giving form to something which never was a quantifiable body, and collectors often feel compelled to state the reasons that motivated them to undertake the task of "collection." The context-specific aspects of colonial folkloristics required the collector to operate in an international and cross-cultural space. Perhaps, therefore, it seems to have been extremely important for "overseas" (Dorson 1968) British folklore collectors to state the motive of their act—collecting and compiling folklore of colonized subjects.

It is important for us to know what motivated them to collect folklore, because the history of folkloristics tells us that the motives of any folklore collector are closely related to the types of folklore collections they compile. In other words, collection of folklore goes hand-in-hand with collectors' socio-political ideologies. The motives of colonial folklore collectors are also important for us, because out of hundreds of thousands of British residents across the Empire, not more than a hundred actually collected and published folklore of a colony. So, we expect to see what was so unique in their situation or perception that led them to undertake the task.

If the folkloristic activity in the British Empire were to be expressed as a digitally animated visual of the world map, it would look something like this: compilations of folklore from different parts of the world reaching a tiny island in the northern part of the globe, from where they go out again as books, but in this second movement the dissemination does not happen in reverse direction; instead, its movement is largely contained within the European continent, while a small portion makes its way to all other parts of the world. If we follow the study of this animated visual by statistics we will know that by the end of nineteenth century England had the largest storehouse of folklore collections from all across the world. If we move from statistics to the actual printed volumes we will see that behind this macro-level phenomenon are individual names and their micro-level realizations of philological and anthropological needs of an Empire spread across the globe. The reasons were born in the specific context of each collector concerned, but were closely related to the notion of the Empire. The motives of these collectors expressed in the pages of the volumes they wrote from colonies on different continents bring forth responses of individuals to historic situations and opportunities. No collector ever really chose the region of his or her folklore collection—it was determined by the facts of their "posting" at a certain "station," "cantonment," or "mofussil town" in a colony or dominion or protectorate of Britain.

The region of collection was the place where the collectors were or had been residents for a while. When we find collectors who published more than one volume and for more than one reason, then while we follow their works we are also following their career graphs and postings. Alice Dracott's first collection (1896) is from central India, where her husband was posted as a civil servant, and the second (1906) is from Simla[1]—the "summer capital" of British India. Richard Carnac Temple wrote about Punjab, Burma, the Andaman and Nicobar Islands, and about his neighborhood in England. These places also represented his first, second, and third important postings, and lastly his retirement years. He fixed his gaze on the surroundings of his residence wherever in the world he happened to be. Robert Sutherland Rattray's long service years in Africa are reflected in two major works, on Chinyanja (1907) and Hausa (1913) folklores. John Roscoe stayed many years in Africa before publishing his renowned work *The Baganda* (1911). "The Rev. John Roscoe reached Buganda in November 1891, and during the next two decades he was both a witness and an accessory to the westernization of the ruling clique of Baganda chiefs. Among those chiefs, Sir Apolo Kagwa, K.C.M.G., the long-time Katikkiro of Buganda, became a close personal friend," says

John Rowe in his review of the second edition of *The Baganda* (Rowe 1967, 164). R. E. Dennett's vast knowledge came from his extensive trade-related travels in Africa. We shall see in the following discussion that in the colonial context "the place" (read the colony) where the collectors were itself became a motive for folklore collection. The nature of the gaze, too, more often than not, changed along with the place. It would not be wrong to say that in most cases the change was marked by an increasing maturity in method and interpretation.

In the overall time frame of British colonial folkloristics, it is around the middle of the nineteenth century that the collections of folklore from non-European colonies started making their appearance in English translations. Mary Frere is chronologically the first collector, publishing her compilation of Indian folktales, *Old Deccan Days,* in 1868. She can also be considered the first folklore collector of the British Empire for two reasons: one, her collection was composed of "folktales," not mythological stories directly connected to religious rituals as in some earlier cases; two, it inspired a number of people to become folklore collectors, as is evident in the spate of folklore collections that followed (Stokes 1879, Steel and Temple 1884). The first collection of African folklore in English made its appearance in 1854, compiled by the German missionary Wilhelm Koelle, followed by the works of another German settler in South Africa, Dr. Wilhelm Heinrich Immanuel Bleek. The first collection of African folklore by a British collector, Rev. Cannon Callaway, appeared in 1871. Collections of folklore from colonies in Africa became a regular feature only in the first decade of the twentieth century. The galaxy of folklore collectors from India is constituted by Richard Carnac Temple (military officer), Mary Frere (governor's daughter), William Crooke (administrator/civil servant), and Rev. Charles Swynnerton (missionary), although there are as many others who will be discussed in the following chapters. The renowned collectors of African folklore are Mary Kingsley (traveler), John Roscoe (missionary), Robert Sutherland Rattray (administrator), John Weeks (missionary), R. E. Dennett (trader), Edwin W. Smith (missionary), and Andrew Dale (administrator), but many others are as important and are included in this work. Only some of the collectors are quoted below—those that express a unique motivation. In some other texts either the motives are mentioned more indirectly or are the repetition of the most common: to sketch out a cultural identity for a group of colonized subjects.

I will present the subject of motivations of colonial collectors in two parts. In the first part I will place the motivations in the words of the collectors without interruption by my analysis, comments, or associated information. All associated information and some comments on the collectors are placed in the endnotes. By this method I hope to draw the reader into the overall mind-set and paradigm of colonial folklorists and their motivations. It will help us to juxtapose them to each other, and the reader may draw her own conclusions. The first part is divided into "Motives in India" and "Motives in Africa." In the second part of the discussion on motives, I will analyze the motivations of the collectors with reference to the macro-level context of British colonial folkloristics.

MOTIVES IN INDIA

Mary Frere

". . . as they [tales] appeared in themselves curious illustrations of Indian popular tradition, and in the hope that something might thus be done to rescue them from the danger of oral transmission" (Frere 1868 [1929], viii).[2]

Flora Anne Steel

"Here we are in a Panjabi village. . . . It is sunset. . . . The boys, half hidden in clouds of dust, drive the herds of gaunt cattle and ponderous buffaloes to the thorn-hedged yards. The day is over—the day which has been so hard and toilful [sic] even for the children,—and with the night comes rest and play. . . . Yet, in spite of this, the hours, though dark, are not dreary, for this, in an Indian village, is *story-telling time*; . . . and from one crowded nest after another rises a childish voice telling some tale, old yet ever new,—tales that were told in the sunrise of the world, and will be told in its sunset" (Steel and Temple 1884, 2–4, italics in original).[3]

Georgiana Kingscote

"Probably further research will lay bare many still hidden treasures of Hindoo folklore; but this small collection of tales will doubtless suffice to throw light on Indian tradition, and to bring forward the natural peculiarities of the Hindoos as well as the assimilation of the folklore of different nations, an assimilation which I maintain, results from the propensities of each country and not from appropriation" (Kingscote 1890, xii).[4]

Alice Elizabeth Dracott

"From their [tales'] cradle under the shade of ancient deodars, beside the rocks, forests and streams of the mighty Himalayan mountains, have I sought these tales to place them upon the great Bookshelf of the World" (Dracott 1906, xi).[5]

Rev. Charles Swynnerton

"For men and women doomed from week to week to live laborious days, for busy merchant and leisureless professional man, for readers of ease and culture whether in the East or in the West, for old folks sitting snug and warm in the chimney-corner, and above all for the young, for boys and girls freed from the term's weary round, this volume of stories is published" (Swynnerton 1892, xv).[6]

Rev. J. Hinton Knowles

"My primary object in collecting these tales was to obtain some knowledge of Kashmírí, which is a purely colloquial language; my secondary object was to ascertain something of the thoughts and ways of the people. Lately I have been contributing some of these tales to the pages of an Indian journal; and now, prompted by the advice of those whose advice I especially value, I venture to publish the whole collection in a book, and thus save them from the clutches of oblivion, to which they would otherwise have been consigned" (Knowles 1888, v–vi).[7]

Rev. E. M. Gordon

"As I have moved amongst the people in the plains and in the jungle, in the rice-fields and in forest land, I have not forgotten that I was a teacher, while I have endeavoured to be a ready learner, and by learning I have become more efficient in teaching.... It is because I have learnt to know them [people], that I now desire to write about them, for I am confident that more information will lead to more interest on their behalf. This book is sent forth with a threefold object: First, that it may add in some small measure to the data which the students of mankind are always glad to receive in order to pursue their own special investigations; secondly, to help officers of the Government and others, who come for the first time to the district, to a better understanding of the people and their ways; thirdly, to enable those who greatly desire the spread of the religion of Christ in India to acquire a more intelligent idea of the beliefs of the people in the villages" (Gordon 1909, vi–vii).[8]

Richard Carnac Temple

"... you will find bards still wandering over the countryside by the score, so the harvest to be gathered is a very large one" (Temple 1883/1962, vii).[9]

"Just as physiologists are enabled by a minute examination of skulls and teeth or hair and so on to differentiate or connect the various races of mankind, so should Folklorists, as in time I have no doubt they will, be able to provide reliable data towards a true explanation of the reasons why particular peoples are mentally what they are found to be. Folklore then as a scientific study has a specific object and occupies a specific place" (Temple 1883/1962, viii).

MOTIVES IN AFRICA

Augustus F. Mockler-Ferryman

"... in laying before the reader some of the folktales of the country, we hope to enable him to compare the mental condition of the native of these parts with that of other savages. A primitive country like West Africa offers to the student of folk-lore much that is interesting, since he finds actually in existence customs and beliefs which, among more civilized people, are merely the survivals of derelict beliefs and ancient traditions. A few centuries hence, doubtless the present religious ideas of the Negro will have been relegated to the domains of folk-lore pure and simple, though there will be little difficulty, with the plethora of literature on the subject, in solving many of the various mysteries" (Mockler-Ferryman 1900, 455).[10]

C. H. Armitage in his Introductory Note to A. W. Cardinall, 1920

"In these days, when the phenomenon generally termed 'civilisation' is extending, to a greater or lesser degree, over the Continent of Africa, there is a growing tendency, that appears not only among the natives themselves, to lose sight of the inner significance of the old-established native customs, which will, in course of time, inevitably disappear or become myths and 'old wives' tales'" (Cardinall 1920, v).[11]

Ruth Fisher

"This book is a feeble attempt to gather from the ashes of the past, some record of the dark ages when Africa was yet unpenetrated and unknown" (Fisher 1911, vii).[12]

R. E. Dennett

"One of the most hopeful signs of the times in Nigeria is that natives (who, by the way, owe their education to the missionaries) are beginning to look upon their native lore in a more serious light than their dear old masters did" (Dennett 1910, vii–viii).[13]

Roland S. Fletcher

"This little book claims to be nothing more than the contents, revised and classified, of a notebook in which between the years 1904 and 1910 Hausa words and phrases hitherto unpublished were noted down wherever heard during my stay in Northern Nigeria. They are published in the hope that students of Hausa may find them useful in the attainment of a more perfect knowledge both of the spoken language and of the native's mental and physical modes of recreation" (Fletcher 1912, 5).

Rev. Edwin Smith and Captain Andrew Dale

"Finding ourselves among a people that were almost unknown to the outside world, we threw ourselves into a study of their language and customs, our motive being, not the production of a book of this kind, but simply that we might prosecute our callings as missionary and magistrate to the best advantage. For whether one is to teach or govern, one's first duty is to understand the people. In the course of years we found our stock of information accumulating, and in 1909 we determined to collaborate in a book that should record the results of our research. From that time we continued our investigations deliberately with that end in view" (Smith and Dale 1920, ix).[14]

D. R. Mackenzie

"The task has been undertaken largely at the request of some of the leading men of the tribe, who are alive to the fact that the old days are passing, even among the conservative Konde, and that, if a record is to be made at all, it must be made without delay" (Mackenzie 1925, xi).[15]

Robert Sutherland Rattray

"On first proceeding to West Africa (the Gold Coast), and on commencing a study of the Hausa language, the compiler of this work was struck by the comparatively high standard of education found among the Hausa MĀLMAI or scribes . . ." (Rattray 1913, viii).[16]

COLLECTORS AND EMPIRE

Motives of folklore collectors play an important role in the way they will approach the subjects—the narrators and the narratives—and the way they will present them to the readers. The motives of individual collectors are related to their historical context, yet it is open to question how far the individual motives are representative of a historical need. This question gains in significance in the case of "pioneer" folklorists, because they have influenced paradigms of folklore research and institutionalization of the discipline of its study in certain directions. Colonial British folklorists were pioneers in their own fields of folklore collection. Their motivations determined the tenor of folklore scholarship all across the British Empire.

In the colonial context, there are many circles of motivations—from macro to micro level, and from state to individual level. Before we go on to the specifics of the macro and micro levels, it is noteworthy that the individual motivations of colonial collectors do not precede the establishment of the colonial state in a particular country but follow it. This differs from the case of nationalist folklorists within Europe, whose work preceded the establishment of the nation-state. The collection and study of folklores of the colonies came into existence once Britain's control over the country concerned was firmly established. This is true of Africa, South Asia, and Australia. Wars had been won, local authorities had been subjugated, and people had come under direct administrative control of the British authorities. At the beginning and around the peak of colonial folklore scholarship nationalist movements or freedom struggles in the colonies had not yet become strong enough to challenge the Empire. As these movements gained momentum, the British passion of collecting folklore waned. The majority of the folklore collections were, therefore, compiled in "peace times," when military and political conflicts were subdued and people from either side had to face each other on a daily basis.

Most of the British collectors worked individually (not withstanding the native assistants), but a few did so in association with other British colleagues. Their motivations are important because they were not professional folklorists, nor did the colonial state ever make it obligatory for its officials to indulge in this activity. Nonetheless, their collections were supported by the state and other organizations.

In his presidential address to the Folk-Lore Society in 1900, E. Sidney Hartland gave words to the situation on both sides of the colonial divide: "The unparalleled changes wrought by the nineteenth century have swept away much. . . . Whatever the twentieth century may do over the rest of the world, it will in Britain at least complete the work of the nineteenth. The muse of folklore is inexorable as the sibyl. Of no other science are the materials disappearing so rapidly" (Hartland 1901, 40). In this situation the "pressing" task was the "work of collection." The urgency in Hartland's writing cannot be missed, and gives the impression that folklore collection had something akin to other colonial "collections" of different kinds of wealth. And because folklore too is seen as wealth, therefore, there is a competition with other nations as folklore collectors. One other European power, namely Germany, worried England even in the area of anthropological and folkloristic research, especially in Africa. Hartland presents figures: ". . . German government, clearer in perception and more prompt in execution than ours, spent in the year 1898 upon anthropological explorations no less a sum than £25,000" (Hartland 1901, 39). The motivations for collecting folklore certainly did not come from individuals alone, but from the states concerned. Hartland, as president of the Folk-Lore Society, was cautioning the imperial British state not to "miss the opportunity" (ibid., 40) of collecting oral lore of the different peoples brought under the British Empire. A year later, in 1901, the Society's President Brabrook, in his condolence note on the death of Queen Victoria, recounted the way folklore studies had grown along with the Empire in Victoria's reign and the Society's contribution therein. "Upon all these grounds, the members of the Folk-Lore Society claim a special share in the universal grief" (Brabrook 1901, 98).

Two reasons for collecting stories were common across the different locales—one, to save and store orality for use in the future; two, to formulate handy definitions of the culture, history, and mentality of the people under consideration. The apparent importance of these tasks gave the collectors a sense of their own importance in the colonial project. Motives of the colonial folklore collectors are less an expression of their folkloristic—that is, their scientific—intent, and more of a record of how they saw themselves. There were clearly three kinds of self-perceptions: British collector as preserver of that which the natives themselves could not preserve; as entertainer back at home with the narration of exotic stories from faraway lands; as creator of archives of knowledge that would further create knowledge and also influence the state policy. The consciousness of these roles let the folklore collectors see themselves as *someone more than* an official, a missionary, or a spouse. The intention or the motive does not determine the overall quality of the work, but does determine its organization and style of narration.

It was the need of the colonizing nation to get to know the people it had brought under its control, and this need motivated the state to "support" the individual efforts in a variety of ways—above all, by granting recognition. The recognition came in several forms, primarily in the officer concerned becoming known as knowledgeable about particular colonies. When need arose, they could be called in as consultants to the state. For example, Rattray was called upon to play a major role in the golden stool controversy among the Ashanti people; Richard Carnac Temple was invited to deliver the inaugural lecture at the establishment of the Anthropology Department at the University of Cambridge; and William Crooke's anthropological questionnaire became an important source for the formation of census categories in India. Diverse actors attached to institutions of state, religion, and education desired collection of folklore of the colonies. Among these were academic institutions, church organizations, and publishers which directly and indirectly motivated individuals to collect folklore. In addition to this was a common and widespread curiosity about "unknown" peoples, which translated into the presence of readers from different walks of life in Britain. Another reason for the popularity of these works was expressed by Lewin: "novelty is as attractive now as ever it was, even in the day when the Athenians went about hearing or telling of some new thing. I think, therefore, that no apology is needed in introducing to English readers races of people, and whose customs have never before been described" (Lewin 1870, 1). Nascent forms of touristic impulse and consumer culture are apparent here and can also be seen as motives for yet other purposes.

The British collectors of Indian and African folklore were generally middle-class educated men and women, like their European counterparts. "The first to pay attention to the lore of the simple folk in India were the well-educated British ladies and gentlemen of the colonial administration," says Heda Jason (1983, 105), and the same could be extended to the colonies in Africa, although missionaries might take chronological precedence (Dorson 1968, 349). Unlike their European counterparts in countries like Germany, they were not poets, philosophers, and philologists, but administrators, missionaries, and dependent women (daughters and spouses of officers). They were collecting folklore in cultures different from their own. We will see that the discourse of the folklore collectors is so full of the hardships they encountered that it hides the actual power they had over peoples and lands. And this was not the power of individuals like early missionaries, or adventurous traders, but the power of the state, invested in the authority of the individual. This applies directly to the officials or civil servants or bureaucrats who were one of the major pillars of British colonial rule, but it also applies to the secure position of the missionaries, traders, and women at this stage, toward the later part of the nineteenth and early part of the early twentieth centuries, when the state's control over the foreign land of their residence was decisive.

There are broadly two kinds of reasons for collecting stories that could be considered "objective" or "contextual" reasons: philological and anthropological. Philological reasons were based on the linguistic needs of the Empire. The colonial officers were working in different linguistic zones and the ability to understand the languages was a necessity. Even after the establishment of the colonial administration and the spread of English language education, the need to know the local languages was never satiated. Folktales could be the easiest ways of learning a language. One of the early language books to teach Persian to the officers of the East India Company, in the late eighteenth century, was a compilation called *Pleasant Stories* by Gilchrist. These were popular stories narrated to him by his teacher of Persian in Calcutta. Knowing local languages could be the key to everything. However, the phase of folklore collection that we are discussing is not about such books, but those claimed to be genuine records of the oral narratives of different peoples. It is interesting that first of all "folktales" were seen as texts that made language readily accessible because they carried accessible ideas, and were then seen as exotic vessels of "other" culture. The philological need here was connected to the anthropological need, that is, as part of the study of man, and folklore herein could be seen as the study of the mind of the communities. While elaborating on the definition of folklore formulated by William John Thoms in 1846 as "the learning of the people," Charlotte Burne says in 1914, "In short, it [folklore] covers everything which makes part of the mental equipment of the folk as distinguished from their technical skill.... Folklore, in fact, is the expression of the psychology of early man, whether in fields of philosophy, religion, science, and medicine, in social organization and ceremonial, or in the more strictly intellectual regions of history, poetry, and other literature" (Burne 1914, 2). Burne's *Handbook of Folklore* was an expression of collective wisdom gained by British folklorists in different colonies, and she was trying to make her comments applicable as far (literally) as the limits of the British Empire. Her definition shows the close link with anthropological inquiry, and yet an attempt to distinguish "folklore" from material culture. I am concerned mainly with the works belonging to the last category; namely, of "strictly intellectual regions of history, poetry, and other literature." This constituted a very important reason for the colonial collectors, because knowing the mind of the people was even more essential for successful administration than knowing their language. Even so, these two types of "objective" or "contextual" needs that motivated many collectors—philological and anthropological—were not always the direct cause of individual folklore collections. The motivations of the folklore collector are small and uniform in their expression when compared to the vast variety of methods employed by them to textualize oral lores of different peoples and the seriousness of the interpretations the collectors derived from the materials they collected.

CHAPTER 3

Method

The Striving of Colonial Folklorists

Devising a method to collect folklore was the most important step in the colonial context, as "method" involved establishing a communication across boundaries of language and culture. In the process of collection, issues of race, power, and violence came into play—a process that Walter Mignolo has termed "coloniality." METHOD used to compile a collection of folklore was everything, not because it was strictly defined, but because it was not possible to define it at the scale of the Empire. Every collector was faced with a unique situation, brought to the task distinctive skills, and had to work out his or her method in this particular context. Method was the precondition to begin approaching the subject of songs and narratives. In the act of collection, method became the preoccupation of every collector. It determined the route along which the documentation proceeded. At the end, method had to be stated as a mark of authenticity. The statement on method created the particular appeal of each work, its value and status on the scale of scientific and popular books. Method was important, because it could be the key to what was being sought through the collection of folklore: the thoughts in the minds of the colonized subjects.

Method was important and also the most difficult aspect of the colonial folklore scholarship. It was easier to wish to collect the folklore of the country or region or linguistic community that a British colonial administrator or missionary had come across, but documenting the oral lore had to be a conscious and long, drawn-out process of transformation of orality into writing. The challenges presented by the context were met with innovation in the field of folklore collection. These challenges of the colonial field are present until now in the form of many current issues of folkloristics—for example, issues of interculturality, multilinguality, race relations, and of ethics in folklore research. The colonial innovations in method can also be seen as nascent forms of dealing with these issues.

In the variety of colonial methods of folklore collection, certain methods were more closely determined by real possibilities than others, while some were amazingly inimitable. This variety matches the varied contexts of the colonial collectors. Yet, some factors were common to all colonial British collectors. Each and every colonial collector was obviously collecting folklore of a foreign tongue. Their writings show that almost all of them knew the language concerned only to a limited extent. In almost no case was the knowledge of the language extensive enough to allow for the independent collection of folklore. The aim of every collector was to publish the collection in the English language. Transcribed, transliterated, and translated folklore from many different languages was finding its international identity in the English tongue, and as such every collector was contributing to increase in the narrative and poetic resources of the English language. To become that resource, however, folklore(s) of the colonized subjects had to get across from narrators to collectors.

Recording orality simultaneously involves the act of hearing. Regina Bendix correctly points out that in folklore studies we have paid much too little attention to "hearing," although the whole process of transformation is based on "hearing" and converting the heard word into the written word.[1] The importance of hearing gains in complexity when the collector does not really understand the tongue of the narrator, or understands it to a limited extent, or does not understand the cultural discourse around the narrator, narratives, and performance—as in the colonial context. This feature cannot be considered a simple deficiency of colonial folkloristics, because it is further combined with the logic of real power relations in the process of documentation and was believed by the collectors to have been overcome by devising a METHOD to do so. Method was the answer to the challenges of the situation. Method, which could not be learned from contemporary European folklorists within Europe.

"Hearing" and "writing" in the colonial context of folkloristics were separated by the same thousands of miles that separated the lands of the narrators and collectors. A journey from "hearing" to "writing" had to cross many boundaries. "It [the narration] was all good to listen to—impossible to put on paper," say Smith and Dale (1920, 336). "Hearing" is the crucial link between oral narratives and their written versions. We will see how this necessary step of the process was methodically worked out in colonial folkloristics. In the following pages we will discuss many different ways that the collectors invented to cross the barrier of one or more foreign languages and unknown cultures.

In addition, the linguistic policy across the British Empire was to teach English to the natives, instead of learning the local languages, and to create native clerks and others to carry on the work of the imperial government under the instructions of the handful of British officers. Though obvious connections between this policy and the general lack of expertise in local languages among the British folklore collectors cannot be established, yet the influence of it is visible in the incapacity of the British officers in languages of the Empire and the availability of the native assistants with knowledge of English. This factor became one of the integral parts of colonial folklore compilations and we shall see in the following pages the extent to which this could be an effective mechanism.

The idea of folklore collection was based on contact with colonized people and an exposure to their oral expressive cultures. As mentioned in the last chapter, this contact extended from the household to the public sphere. From *ayahs* to office clerks, the colonial officers, their family members, and the missionaries depended on the natives in all areas of life and living. The political, economic, and social reality of colonial rule expressed itself in every moment of existence, and the power positions had to be expressed and maintained on a daily basis. It is probably not just a coincidence that the first folklore collection from the Empire was compiled from the stories narrated by an ayah, because this relationship—between the ayah and her young adult ward—was probably the "closest" in the colonial context, and storytelling was one of its main activities. British women collected folklore from domestic servants, missionaries from their parishes, and officials from the people that came under their administration. The writing of any collector reveals that the choice of the narrative traditions she or he documented and the narrators from whom these had to be heard were invariably connected to the daily performance of the role of the colonial officers, women, and missionaries. No officer set his heart on documenting the folklore of any region for any other reason, say "interest based on information," but solely on the circumstantial contact with a certain region and people. This motivating factor which was both coincidental (not every woman felt interested in recording the narratives of domestics, nor every missionary of his parish, nor every official of people under his administration) and systematic (women came in contact with a certain set of natives, while officials and missionaries had wider contact) determined, to some extent, the method that would be followed in the collection of narratives. And yet, no two collectors followed exactly the same method across the colonial Empire.

All of the colonial British collectors, no matter how different their contexts and methods were, faced two common factors that I will call *problems of language* and *privileges of power*. The two—*problems* and *privileges*—constitute an enigmatic combination for collection of folklore that expresses itself in the variety of methods employed in the colonial world. Only one of these factors—the problems of language—was recognized and articulated by the colonial collectors. The second factor—privileges of power—was apparently assumed by the collector, requiring no articulation; but it runs through the execution of any method. It is a factor in this analysis because it is central to the very existence of colonial folklore scholarship. What we need to define is: what are these privileges of power? Difference of class between folklore collectors and narrators is a universal feature of folkloristics, so how do the privileges of power of colonial collectors differ from social privileges of other collectors, say of the Grimms, with regard to their narrators? The colonial privileges of power are not of class, because the hierarchy of class structure too is bound by the entity of the system as a whole. The colonial collector is not in the higher bracket of the native social hierarchies, whatever they were. The colonial collector's position was above the highest bracket of the native hierarchies—above the clansmen, above the tribal chiefs, above the local rulers, above small kings, above the Mughal Emperor, because all those rulers had been subjugated. The colonial collector was of the supra-class that was laying down the systems anew without being bound by the native systems. Individually, any collector was handicapped in many ways, essentially by lack of knowledge about the natives' language and cultural systems. But as bearer of the collective identity of race and nation, the importance of the handicaps was diminished by his or her position.

In the following pages I will discuss the methods used to collect folklore by the British collectors across the colonial Empire, but especially in India and Africa. Richard Dorson exercised two options for systematizing and discussing colonial British folklore collections. The first of these was chronological, and the second was personality based. He created separate chronological records of folklore collections from India, Africa, and Australia in the chapter "Overseas Folklorists" in his book *The British Folklorists* (1967), wherein he also discussed gender and professional identities of the British collectors. So, while a chronological record does not seem required, categorizing colonial folklorists with reference to their gender and professional identities does not serve my analytical purposes, because there are many common elements between methods of different categories of collectors. There are also works produced in association across these categories. Therefore, I would discuss the issue of method under categories that reflect differences in the methods rather than the differences in the collectors. The subject of this chapter is METHOD, not collectors.

The first category, *Folkloristic Methods,* refers to procedures adopted/followed by a large number of collectors with the stated aim of creating an "authentic" and "scientific" record. These were also methods accepted by scholarly institutions in Europe and partially also devised by them. These methods, in different ways, connect up with the mainstream of the history of folkloristics. This section has the widest spectrum of collectors. Most of the colonial collectors claimed to be presenting "authentic" records of the oral lore of one of the colonized subjects of the Empire and detailed out the procedure they followed in order to ensure authenticity. From amateur collectors to the learned officials and occasional professors, all employed a conscious method to record oral narratives from foreign languages and present them in the English language.

The second category is *Amazing Methods,* that is, completely innovative and ingenious ways to record orality. These methods have neither any predecessors nor followers. In this section there are those few collectors who invented an altogether novel way to fulfill the aim of revealing the mind of the natives. There are collectors from all three groups in this category—women, missionaries, and officials.

Third is *"Native" Folklorists of Colonial Archives.* This section discusses "native" associates whose contribution went far beyond than that of "assistance" to colonial British collectors. They were "folklorists" in their own right. The reason for including these in a separate category is that their involvement forged new power structures of method, knowledge, and colonial relations. The native assistants, associates, interpreters, scribes, and others who made significant contributions toward the modern study of folklore have no independent identity. They were all men, from India and Africa, and their record is crucial for any postcolonial understanding of colonial folkloristics. Their record also presents yet unspecified dilemmas faced by folklorists with reference to powers that be. However, this study does not include the native independent, often nationalist folklorists that took over the field after the first quarter of the twentieth century in some of the colonies. The "native" scholars under our discussion are those that worked in different capacities with the British folklore collectors, most often during the peak of colonial rule.

THE FOLKLORISTIC METHODS

To formulate the model of colonial folkloristics it is essential to understand the methods used by colonial British folklore collectors across the world whose works have been valued by folklore scholars. I will discuss "method(s)" in two steps. First, I will present before the reader statements of colonial collectors about their methods. This will let us see what were their major concerns in the process of collecting. Second, I will place these statements in an analytical frame defined by our contemporary perspectives to reach an understanding of colonial method beyond the descriptions of the collectors. I am reading colonial texts like *haiku* poems—that is, with the awareness that something is said, not everything, and that that which is not said is actually as important as that which is said.

Method—As Narrated by Collectors

In this section I will discuss the various methods of folklore collection used and described by colonial British collectors whose works have been considered "scientific" by their contemporaries and later by folklore scholars. The "scientific" nature of folklore collection was essentially the claim to authenticity of the record, and this claim could be made on the basis of method adopted and how that particular method ensured a printed compilation close to the oral version heard by the collector. Collectors who wished to be taken seriously made this claim by detailing the scientific nature of their method. Two of their major concerns were text and performance. The oral text was to be textualized and involved issues of access (to the text), recording, translation, and publication. The "performance" itself was another issue and posed different kinds of challenges toward portrayal. Very often the performance of the narrators had impressed and moved the collectors, and sometimes the collectors tried to portray it. Since "empirical" knowledge was the best claim of colonial collectors, this section will give us glimpses of what they were actually experiencing as folklore performance(s) across the British Empire. For example, the most popular time of storytelling across the British Empire was the evening or night.

Text and Textuality

It all began rather simply: Mary Frere (1868) cajoled her ayah into narrating stories for a record. Anna complied, sitting cross-legged on the floor and narrating stories. Frere did not face the problem of language, as Anna narrated in English, albeit "in her own words of expressive but broken English" (xix). She wrote down the stories and could obviously ask for them to be repeated. She read the written versions to Anna and apparently gained her consent. The first collection of Indian folktales, which was to go into many editions and be translated into fourteen languages within the next two decades, was compiled in the easy and personal atmosphere between the narrator and the collector. Mary Frere's claim to authenticity was based on her apparently congenial and affectionate relationship with the narrator. Frere claimed to have heard the narratives many times and to have cross-checked her versions with the narrator. She topped her claim by providing an autobiographical account of the narrator's life in a separate chapter titled "Narrators's Narrative." It has been noticed since the very first publication of *Old Deccan Days* in 1868 that this account was important in the reception of her work. The autobiographical narrative of Anna Liberata de Souza—the narrator—gave her an identity which no other representation could have given her. It juxtaposed the contemporaneity of narrator and the traditional nature of her narratives. It also expressed the complexity of religious and narrative identity in the colonial context: Anna was a second-generation Christian, but her stories were of Hindu stock. Indeed, in the very first folklore collection from the Empire were certain complexities that would dominate the spate of folklore collections in the last two decades of the century, namely the multilingual and multireligious nature of colonial folkloristics. Yet, Frere's project was as simple as a prototype can be, because it was compiled in an intimate setting where the narrator and the collector knew each other, and the collector could cross-check with the narrator. Frere did not face the severity of the problem of different speeds of speaking and writing—a problem that required expansion of her simple method by others.

Legends of Punjab (1884–1885) was a scientific advance in the collection of oral lore. Richard Carnac Temple (1850–1931) collected a highly stylized genre—the versified legends performed by roaming bards across the northwest Indian state of Punjab. As the region connected India with Afghanistan and thereon to Central Asia, the influence of Persian and Islamic narrative traditions was widespread and the professional singers, *mirasis,* performed versified legends in an array of venues, from village guest houses to palaces.[2] Mirasis were also known to be the keepers of local genealogies and land records. Temple claimed to have seen them performing on various occasions and then summoned some to his official residence and had them narrate the legends. Between summoning and narrating were many steps. Why would the narrators come? Temple tells us that at one level they were interested in obtaining a *chit* from him. A *chit* was a letter of introduction, a note of acknowledgment, or some other item from a British officer that would permit the bearer to approach the officer's successors or colleagues in other government departments, where the narrator might require some help; in short, it would give him a new identity in the colonial world. It is more than likely that handing out the *chit* to the performers was part of Temple's method of forming a viable relationship with the performers of the legends. Narrators also expected to be treated like guests, as they would have been in a village, and therefore to be supplied with food and opium. Temple fulfilled these expectations, even though they did not match with his sensibilities, and he recorded the demand with a condescending attitude, simultaneously saying that the bards were considered people of "ill-repute." Feelings probably remained unexpressed on both sides, but the deal had been struck and the narration began.

Now, when the narration began, it turned out that "the speed of the bard was a problem." Temple had trained Chaina Mull, his office clerk, called a *munshi* in the Raj parlance, for recording the oral narrative, but he could not have written as fast as the narrator spoke. When the narrator was interrupted, he lost the flow of his narration, and slowly his interest in narration. Consequently the narrative may have been curtailed. Temple tried to ascertain completeness by ordering his munshi, Chaina Mull, to remain faithful to the method taught, and believed that the power of his authority delivered the desired results. There are, however, possibilities of many decisions by any and all concerned. Temple did not really understand the language of bards in Punjab. He had learned Persian in his preparation for joining the service in India, but Persian was the language of the Mughal court in India, not of the wandering mirasis. His munshi translated the bard's language into Persian, from which Temple transcribed and translated the text into English. He published the English transcript and translation.

This method, whereby the collector could summon the narrators to narrate especially for him, could be called the official method: "... the only method likely to satisfy the demands of science—is this: the observer must draft word-for-word reports of what he hears; and must further give the original words, when a foreign tongue is used, so that it may be possible independently to control the version" (Rattray 1913, v–vi). What Marrett, an Oxford professor, was writing in his introduction to the administrator Rattray's work was based on the method developed by officials of the colonial Empire in different colonies.

A situation, very similar to that of Temple in India, was faced by Rattray with the Chinyanja and the Hausa peoples in Africa. His experience showed him that the above-mentioned method represented an ideal, not a realistic model. Rattray's text also lets us see the difference between the models that were created in England and the realities of folklore collection in the colonies; the former were rather ignorant about the latter. To that ignorance Rattray's text juxtaposed a picture from the field to show the challenges faced in the execution of the ideal method.

When the witness is illiterate—as commonly happens . . . its [method's] application proves exceedingly troublesome. . . . A more or less formal dictation lesson has somehow to be given and received; and the several parties to it are only too apt to conspire each in his own way to render it a failure. Thus the story-teller, on the one hand, is probably shy and suspicious at the outset; is put out of his stride by the slightest interruption; and, becoming weary all too soon, tends to take short cuts, instead of following to the end the meandering path of the genuine tradition. The reporter, in his turn, is incessantly puzzled by the idiom, more especially since in such a context archaisms will be frequent; boggles over a pronunciation adapted to a monotonous sing-song delivery, or else, perhaps, to a dramatic mimicry carried on in several voices; and is likely to be steadily outpaced into the bargain. (Rattray 1913, vi)

Rattray's account shows that the problem of speed is also the manifestation of the problem of communication between the narrator and the collector. As readers of colonial texts we have only the collector's account to go by, and therefore need to read between the lines. Rattray places the problem squarely on the incapacities of the narrator by saying that because the narrators are illiterate they get confused by the act of writing and the demands of the writer. When faced with the interruptions of the writing, they start changing the progression of the narratives themselves. If so, then we are faced with yet another issue: were the texts collected and presented by the British collectors to the public compromised to an extent that they were summaries of narratives? Or, did the colonial collectors try to resolve this problem, too?

The difference in the speed of speaking and writing was naturally experienced in many cases. The question is—how did this affect the construction and the authenticity of the English text? While Temple and Rattray leave the reader with the impression that they somehow got past the lacunae by use of their authority, Smith and Dale, who published tales of Ila, confessed to a loss:

> *Ask him [the narrator] now to repeat the story slowly so that you may write it. You will, with patience, get the gist of it, but the unnaturalness of the circumstance disconcerts him, your repeated request for the repetition of a phrase, the absence of encouragement of his friends, and, above all, the hampering slowness of our pen, all combine to kill the spirit of story-telling. Hence we have to be content with far less than the tales as they are told. And the tales need effort of imagination to place readers in the stead of the original listeners. (Smith and Dale 1920, 336)*

Smith and Dale give the blame more to "writing" than to the narrators. Just like Temple in India and Rattray in West Africa, Smith and Dale followed a seriously considered method, which they stated as follows:

> *... sixty-one examples of Ila tales, which were almost all written down by one of us from dictation, the only exceptions being those few, not more than six in all, which were written for us by intelligent natives..., we have given them precisely as they were dictated or written, and the translation is as literal as possible consonant with smoothness and intelligibility. They might have been improved by altering the sequence of some sentences and pruning away some of the redundancies, but we did not wish so to retouch them as to obliterate the characteristics of the original. (Smith and Dale 1920, 334)*

The clash between the methodological wishes and prevailing realities is evident in the writings of Smith and Dale. What they say is noteworthy—"as they were dictated or written" and "translation is as literal as possible." So, the final text is at best what the narrator gave in a context in which he was not exactly comfortable. Translators had limits beyond which literal translation was not possible. Smith and Dale, like other collectors, do not reveal the exact nature of their difficulties, as in literal translation, nor the details of their solutions. Smith and Dale admitted that "... they [tales] gradually lose flavour as they pass from the African's telling first into writing and then into a foreign idiom" (Smith and Dale 1920, 336). These collectors insightfully point out that it is not only the knowledge of the language that is required to "fully appreciate them [tales]." For that "one must be familiar, ... with the characteristics of the animals spoken of" [334–35].

Interestingly, Smith and Dale accept the limitation of the written record of oral folklore and propose a futuristic technological solution: "It would need a combination of phonograph and kinematograph [*sic*] to reproduce a tale as it is told" [336]. Smith and Dale were writing in the age of silent cinema, and probably could not even dream of the convenience of digital camcorders. Technological problems specific to colonial folklore scholarship were connected even to printing.

To tell a tale as it was told is a noble aim, but in the colonial context it was realized in a variety of ways. Rev. Roscoe had an interesting resolve. Roscoe was the writer of the first part of the Mackie Ethnological Report, a huge document concerning many tribes in Central Africa, and the documentation of their folklore was part of the larger project. "It was Frazer who arranged for Roscoe to embark on the Mackie Expedition to Central Africa (Uganda) in 1919–1920" (Ray 1984, 397). Roscoe tells us about the process in which the record was made:

The investigation was carried out without the use of an English interpreter, though at times it was necessary to appeal to some native who knew a language common to myself and the person under examination. Yet even in these cases all the information came to me through a native medium, uninfluenced by contact with the western mind.[3] *In almost every instance a man of the tribe with which I was dealing, who knew some other native dialect that I understood, became the interpreter, and to him I turned when I was in doubt or failed to understand the language of the tribe under examination. Thus, when the information was not actually first-hand, it was as near to it as possible, for there was no man attached to the expedition who, knowing English, could talk to me and give impressions influenced by western ideas.* (Roscoe 1923, vii, emphasis added)

Rev. Roscoe was a missionary, but his method of research was the one considered "standard" among officialdom. His chose a wide field of research even though his linguistic capability was limited. Roscoe's statement of method presents a typical combination of problems of language and privileges of power. It is noteworthy that Temple's and Roscoe's writings show the journey of each text through many languages—that is, not necessarily a translation between only two languages. The narrator narrates in one language, one or more interpreters translate it into another local language that the folklore collector knows, and the collector then translates it into English. Indeed, it would be impossible to track the changes that would have taken place in this journey. Yet it is interesting that Roscoe sees that the information he provides is not "first-hand" and admits that it is only "as near to it [first-hand] as possible." We could paraphrase his text and say that this is where he is also locating his point of view: as near to the subject as possible. This virtual location of his perspective is authenticated by his physical location in Africa and makes his text worthy of his intended audiences' considerations.

After the problems of speed and literal translation arose the problem of translating concepts and social signifiers. Roscoe gives a more detailed account of his method with regard to his translations: "In this volume I have recorded the findings from a single tribe, the Banyoro, or, as I have called them, the Bakitara, which is their correct name.... I have made no attempt to write any grammatical notes or to make any remarks concerning the language beyond giving a short vocabulary.... I have ... avoided them [local terms] as much as possible and retained our English titles of king, queen, prince, and princess, a procedure which makes the story more readily understood by English readers" (Roscoe 1923, vi–vii). Roscoe's statement shows his concerns with issues of "translatability" and accessibility in the target language and points to the ultimate freedom that the collectors probably felt in deciding the method to represent the subjects of their research: they could decide freely that grammatical notes were not required without giving any reason for it. "Any remarks concerning the language" seem to be really unimportant in Roscoe's eyes, but he does not say why. Could it be that he was incapable of making "any remarks"? Concerning the way his translations had been arrived at, it is unlikely that he was in a position to make those remarks. His authority did not depend on this capacity; it depended on the institutions that had already placed their trust in him. He could replace the terms with those understandable by the English readers. This feature brings in yet another dimension of colonial folkloristics—the language of the British collectors. The ultimate aim of collectors to be read by people in Europe influenced their many choices, including the choice of language in which they would themselves write. Decisions like Roscoe's would have been made by many collectors, and if we consider this feature widespread in colonial folkloristic method, then what we are dealing with is the implementation of cultural hegemony. The colonizer collector and his target readers wanted simply to take out the text from the narrator, from the context of performance, from the art of performance, and finally, even from the social context of the text as embedded in language. The collector's role was often expressed in administrators' language, and the sense of real power over the lives of the narrating subjects often determined the decisions finally taken:

> *I have thought it wise to write of the customs in the past tense because of the transition stage through which the country is passing and the changes now being wrought by the advance of education. It is not, however, intended to*

lead the reader to think that all these customs have passed away, for there are still many people who practise them as of old. Christian missions and a kindly Government have done much to enlighten and restrain, but there are still to be found natives who cling to their old superstitious practices and follow them whenever they can do so without arousing the anger of officers or missionaries. (Roscoe 1923, vii–viii)

Roscoe's method reflects a wish to erase the culture of the native, and it is so strong that it finds a macabre expression in writing. The author decides to use "past tense" because he believes that the life and culture he is documenting is correctly on its way to extinction. Even so, he is unable to wait for the historical process to take shape and attempts to jump the time line by writing about present in past tense.

The problem of language did not come to an end with the collector having devised a method of collection, but continued right up to the stage of printing the book. J. Torrend pointed to one problem, not generally mentioned, but which must have been experienced by many as they were all bringing back materials in different languages:

having to deal with a variety of languages, I have had to face the eternal difficulty of a general alphabet. Lepsius's Standard Alphabet would, it might appear, have served well enough. The fact is that it does not. Printers, especially those in a smaller line of business, find his symbols, ń, ṅ, š, ž, etc., inaccessible, unless it be at prices which do not suit them, particularly when capitals are wanted, or they have to apply to a foundry other than the one they usually deal with, and that is what they do not care to do. (Torrend 1921, 2)

The problems of orthography were different in Africa and in South Asia. In Africa many languages were unwritten, while in South Asia many had long written traditions and well-tailored orthography. At the stage of printing, however, all of them faced similar difficulties. Stuart Blackburn has discussed the history of printing folklore in colonial South India and traced back the developments to the sixteenth century, when Tamil became the first non-European language to appear in print [Blackburn 2003, 31]. And yet "printing presses were difficult to obtain ... and types for Indian scripts were extremely difficult to make: following the successful Tamil experiments in the sixteenth century ..., no new types were cast in India until the early eighteenth century. Paper was also scarce. Indeed, the scarcity of printing presses, types and paper remained a problem, especially for Indians, well into the nineteenth century" [Blackburn 2003, 35]. As such, dissimilarities in colonies were somewhat erased in modern history when their relationship to modern technologies became structured by the same forces of colonialism and more of their folklore was published in English transliteration and translation.

Besides technology, the problem of the different speeds of speaking and writing were rooted in the incapacities of the collectors too, especially in the fact that most were not trained ethnologists. Collectors were conscious of this, and Driberg stated, "Vast lacunae are inevitable, partly owing to my lack of qualifications as an ethnologist, and partly to the circumstances in which the material was collected" (Driberg, 1923, 9) The circumstance was the usual busy life of a colonial administrator, due to which Driberg confessed not having done detailed investigations. As postcolonial readers, our surprise begins at this stage, because after confessing to such fatal problems in the collection, the collector publishes the book with the assurance "however haphazard the method, every care has been taken to exclude all matter, whether ethnological or linguistic, the accuracy of which has not been thoroughly and repeatedly tested and confirmed" (ibid.).

These examples show that the colonial collectors were always searching for method. "Literal translation" was the mantra of this model, but literal translation was anything but easy. The difficulties lay in a number of layered reasons, and the colonial collectors often realized how inadequate the given models were with regard to the complexities of the situation, but were themselves subject to the hegemonic powers of the global design. In the final analysis of their method, they aligned whatever method they had developed to the demands of the "science" as articulated from the platform of the Folk-Lore Society in London. Between devising the method of collection for a local situation and aligning it to a global science was the process in which the method was executed and became the experience of the collector. Once in motion the physical time and space of the performers, performances, and folklores dominated the senses of the collector and became her or his actual experience of folklore in a colony. The narrative of this experience became another constant feature of colonial method.

The narrative of the collectors' experience was not bound by scientific demands. The demands of the science as articulated from London were more concerned with acquiring folklore collected on the same principles across the Empire. It was based on the assumption that folklore everywhere will emerge in the categories identified in Europe. So, what was identified as folktale or fairy tale in a colonized country was not necessarily seen as such by the people who practiced its narration and listening. More importantly, they had their own terms to define these oral texts, but the "science" did not wish to know that. The "science" did not wish to acknowledge the existence of other "sciences." Just as "native" terms for rulers and people were replaced with "king, queen, demon, etc.," most of the Asian, African, Australian, and other aesthetic and scientific categories were not mentioned by colonial British collectors. Colonized subjects had songs and stories that could be decontextualized and reproduced. What those subjects thought about those narratives and songs was pushed under the rubric of "beliefs" with which the European readers need not concern themselves. So, the next step in the colonial method, after the plan to get texts, was to observe the performance and write about what the collector *saw*. (Collectors' ignorance of the languages concerned is worth remembering at this point.) The collectors narrated their experience, or its fragments, and created through it a feel of authenticity. As we discuss the descriptions of supposedly actual performances on various continents, we will consider the following questions: is there a similarity of form in the writings of the collectors, and what kind of information is provided?

Performance and Observation

We know that the process of folklore collection brought the officials in contact with expert storytellers; we will now see how these were portrayed by the collectors.

Smith and Dale, who collected folktales in Northern Rhodesia, were among the few collectors who identified their narrators in some detail. They tell us about a performer and the scene of performance: "One listens to a clever story-teller, as was our old friend Mungalo, from whom we derived many of these tales. Speak of eloquence! Here was no lip-mumbling, but every muscle of face and body spoke, a swift gesture often supplying the place of a whole sentence. He would have made a fortune as a raconteur upon the English stage. The animals spoke each in its own tone: the deep rumbling voice of Momba, the ground hornbill, for example, contrasting vividly with the piping accents of Sulwe, the hare" (Smith and Dale 1920, 336).

This description of one oral narrator makes us acutely aware of the limitations of the printed record. What a collector hears is not just the narrative as a set of dramatic events, but a *narrator* and a particular *narration*. Attempts were made to resolve some of these problems by using Performance Theory and technology in the late twentieth century, but the realization of the problems emerged much earlier. The question is: did the colonial collector try to resolve this? Smith and Dale are among those who undertake to describe the performance, however briefly, for their European readers. They are probably the only ones to write so appreciatively of these performances and tell their readers that the exact pleasure of the live narration will never be communication through "cold print" (Smith and Dale 1920). On the one hand, they seem culturally more perceptive than many others, but on the other hand, their disclaimers seem to be competence claims. Smith and Dale describe the setting and the audience of the narrator further:

> *It is at evening around the fires that the tales are told, especially on dark nights, when the people cannot dance so comfortably. Many of the tales are known far and wide, others in lesser areas. But, however often the people hear them, they never seem weary of repetition. They never say, "Oh, that's an old tale," . . . with no trace of boredom [they] come in with their ejaculations just at the right points, take, it may be, a sentence out of the narrator's mouth, or even keep up a running echo of his words. (Smith and Dale 1920, 336)*[4]

Recording some of the important aspects of oral cultures, Smith and Dale's description also candidly portrays the difference in the act of hearing and reading—the latter being the act through which their European audience would receive the narratives. The printed text is minus all the faculties of the narrators and the culture of listening. Smith and Dale also describe only one of the narrators, without connecting him to the exact texts in their volume that he narrated, and many others they heard and saw remain without a written record about themselves.

Although it is futile to pose this question because the possibility of getting an answer is nil, yet I ask: in the totality of the context, did the narrators not imagine that they too were being recorded along with their narratives? My guess is that many might have thought they were being recorded as personalities. It is obvious that their wishes did not matter and that they represented for the collector storehouses of folklore, even though among narrators were self-conscious professional artists and not only those who did not cultivate an identity as narrators.

Clement Doke came more directly to the subject of folklore while writing on his collection of the folktales of the Lamba: "The Lamba people, like all Bantu tribes, are remarkably rich in their store of folk-lore; numbers of fundamental tales are found in almost every Bantu dialect" (Doke 1927, XII). He gives a vivid account of the oral performance of narratives among the Lamba:

> *In order to hear these folk-tales effectively, one must hear them in their native setting. The native is happiest and most communicative in the evening after the substantial meal of the day when the thought of hot sun, a long, heavy march, and a hungry stomach has been banished under the beneficent influence of a crackling log fire and a great heap of stiff "inshima" porridge in the hastily constructed zareba. Overhead is an inky-black sky dotted with brilliant stars, a slight breeze is moving the tops of the trees, and all is silent save the regular gurgling noise of the calabash pipes, as the men sit or lie around the numerous camp fires within the stockade. Then the narrator will refill his pipe, and start his story: "Mwe w̄ame!" ("Mates!"), and at once they are all attention. After each sentence he pauses automatically for the last few words to be repeated or filled in by his audience, and as the story mounts to its climax, so does the excitement of the speaker rise with gesture and pitch of voice.... To reproduce such stories with any measure of success, a gramophone record together with a cinematograph picture would be necessary. The story suffers from being put into cold print, and still more does it suffer in being translated into the tongue of a people so different in thought and life. (Doke 1927, XIII)*

Doke echoes Smith and Dale almost exactly. It is noteworthy how abstract these accounts are and how little concrete information can be deduced from this description. It seems from the description that the narrator and his listeners were perhaps porters in a long march, and told stories at the end of a hard working day. Then the collector gives us the briefest possible description of the narrator and the audience. This certainly could not have been the only time that the collector experienced storytelling, nor the only narrator, yet the collector systematically does not talk specifics of any individual performance or variety of setting.

Dennett also comments on the current and changing situation of folklore. As cited in the previous chapter, Dennett sees it as an influence of missionary education that has made the "natives" consider their lore "in a more serious light." He also names "native" individuals who were compiling folklore: "Bishop Johnson gave us a little work on Yoruba paganism.... Bishop Phillips wrote a little book called *Ifa*. The Rev. Lijadu has given us Ifa and Orunanila. Mr. Sobo wrote Arofa odes or poems. Dr. Johnson has lectures on Yoruba history.... Mr. Adesola is now engaged in writing a most interesting account of Yoruba Death and Burial Secret Societies, which are appearing in the Nigerian Chronicle" (Dennett 1910, viii). This comment points to the process of "modernity" in the colonies, even though it is debatable whether the changes under way should be termed modernity or westernization, but evident is the change of perception of the colonized people toward their lore, which was now termed "traditional," increasingly dissociated from the processes of living and displaced along with the people from its familiar locales. British rule had brought another world-view, which was integrated deep into the societies concerned through "education." "Education" was one of the main pillars of British colonial rule that influenced cultural changes in a major way, including the perceptions of the native collectors of folklore we shall discuss later in this chapter.

Most collectors spared even fewer words with regard to their narrators. While a note on the method of translation was more or less mandatory, it seems to have been equally not-required to mention the names of narrators, the place of narration and recording, and any sociological data about the narrators apart from the mention of their poverty. This absence is so widespread in colonial folklore collections that it appears to be systematic rather than incidental. If this system was not articulated, then it was engrained in the minds of the collectors through their own education and belief. The peculiar hierarchies of the colonial worlds, mentioned earlier, came into play the moment a British resident in a colony decided to contact professional storytellers. It is interesting to know how someone with an attitude of superiority like Roscoe would have contacted his humble narrators. Roscoe acknowledges certain kinds of help: "The king of Bunyoro was most helpful and spent hours of his time in recounting what he remembered of the court as it was in his father's day. He also procured for me those men who had the most intimate knowledge of the customs of the country, and he arranged a week's pageant of the ceremonies of old, thus enabling me to secure photographs which I could not otherwise have obtained" (Roscoe 1923, ix).

Apparently, as a visiting official, conducting a state-funded survey, Roscoe was being entertained by the local rulers and a type of folklore research was emerging that would become the staple of postcolonial state ceremonies: "procuring" natives from a hinterland and organizing a "pageant of the ceremonies." Performance pushed to the margins of history and invited to present itself in an artificial context: narratives that are totally for opposite occasions, like birth and death, or those performed far apart from each other in the course of a year, could now be performed one after another in a week-long festival of sorts, a "festival of ceremonies," including narrative performance. In an earlier work, too, Roscoe had followed an almost similar methodology:

I owe a debt of gratitude to my friend, Sir Apolo Kagwa, K.C.M.G., Prime Minister and Regent of Uganda, in whose house most of my information was collected. He spared no pains to bring old people whom I should otherwise have failed to see, and who would have refused to give information to an Englishman, had not Sir Apolo induced them to do so. Often Sir Apolo had men carried sixty and sometimes a hundred miles, and entertained them for several weeks at a time that I might have opportunities of seeing and questioning them, and writing out their accounts. Through Sir Apolo's kindness, too, I have been able to see priests and mediums from most of the old temples, and the principal men from each clan, from whom I have been able to take notes of the customs which were peculiar to their clans, and to gain a better understanding of the general customs of all the clans. Again, medicine-men versed in the past customs have been brought to me and warned to speak the truth and hide nothing. In addition to this Sir Apolo himself has not only placed his large store of knowledge at my disposal, but has been ever ready to prosecute the most careful enquiry into any difficulty that arose in the path of investigation. It is sad to think that only one or two of the numerous men with whom I spent hours of happy work are alive, the others have passed away. (Roscoe 1911, x–xi)

These passages testify to the actual distance between the narrators and the collectors. The collectors did not know their language, and could not even reach them except through the ruling classes of the native society. In his review of the 1965 reprint volume of Roscoe's *The Baganda*, John Rowe informs us, "The Rev. John Rosoce reached Buganda in November 1891, and during the next two decades he was both a witness and an accessory to the westernization of the ruling clique of Baganda chiefs. Among those chiefs, Sir Apolo Kagwa, K.C.M.G., the long-time Katikkiro of Buganda, became a close personal friend.... Despite the determination of both men to change the traditional religious and political system of the Baganda, each in his own way was fascinated by that system" (Rowe 1967, 164). Rowe further elaborates upon Roscoe's method: "Kagwa made searching enquiries among the old men acquainted with life in Buganda before the penetration of European influences. These knowledgeable elders were brought to the capital and based in the Katikkiro's official residence for weeks at a time. It was here that Roscoe met them and conducted the many lengthy interviews which produced the information for his own book. In his preface, Roscoe pointed out that these elderly informants knew no English and were therefore free from alien influence. But he did not make clear whether their answers were at all influenced by the Katikkiro. In order to gauge the reliability of *The Baganda* for modern historians, the attitudes of both Rosoce and Kagwa must be taken into consideration" (Rowe 1967, 164).

And Roscoe was not the only one to resort to this method. Richard Carnac Temple in Punjab, India, used the Indians in his office staff to summon the narrators. Rev. Swynnerton recorded narratives in the same region sitting in the house of a British civil servant friend in Peshawar. William Crooke asked a civil services' colleague who was director of the Public Instructions Department to send a circular to village school teachers across the province to send tales to Crooke.

Traces of resistance on the part of natives are clearly visible in Roscoe's texts quoted above. The "native" performers transfer their knowledge not without reluctance and after being asked for it in some way or another by their traditional authority—their own rulers. This also points to the willingness of certain groups within colonized societies to help a British official or missionary to collect folklore. Roscoe portrays the Kattikiro as an intellectual as engaged in salvage-operation as Roscoe. This willingness is not so apparent in the case of narrators. Another irony is, however, more masked: these medicine men, diviners, and priests were the very people who had been banished to the hinterland, banned from practicing their beliefs, arts, or crafts. The expression and practice of their knowledge system was central to the African tribal societies, but they had been made dysfunctional under charges of following superstitious, unscientific practices. Colonial rule was now interfering with their knowledge yet again, this time by compelling them to perform it for a written record after having been made to accept its extinction from the reality. Versions of this reality existed in other locales, too. In South Asia certain performance traditions were ostracized as black magic. In other cases, where the narrators were not stigmatized, the collector was not concerned with the narrators or their actual existence, work, and suffering. The distance—in every sense of the word—between the narrators and collectors was immense and could be called a *colonial gulf*. This colonial gulf could only be negotiated with the involvement of "native" rulers, officials, and intelligentsia.

From the above analysis of the "folkloristic method" it is apparent that there are many common elements in the descriptions of method(s) by different colonial collectors. The collectors were placed far away from each other and were in inimitably different contexts, yet their varied methods are akin to each other. It is *as if* they share a method code. And if there is a code, then it needs to be broken to know what it contains. In other words, descriptions of method by different colonial collectors have been accepted by subsequent scholars and have become the bases of their evaluation. An acceptance based on the code that emerges from the descriptions of the British colonial collectors is by now certainly redundant, even if it were acceptable when Dorson wrote his genealogy of British folklorists (1967). Postcolonial theory and history render that kind of genealogy a purposeless project. I suggest that this "code" is to be treated like a *haiku* text; then one needs to hear that which is not said. This is possible because that which is not said is often present in what is said. So, in the next part—The Amazing Method—we will reconsider the descriptions of the collectors so as to read what has not been written, but is present in what is written. This reading is aimed at reaching the complete text of colonial folkloristic method. "The Amazing Method" is not a mere critique of the code, but the step to reach a historically possible and intellectually feasible model that could be called colonial folkloristics.

Colonial Methods from Postcolonial Perspective

The method considered "scientific" in its own time, acknowledged by academic institutions, meaningful to the history of folkloristics, and followed by different kinds of collectors was based on the descriptions of the collectors and the suggestions of colleagues in England. If we reconsider these texts we will realize that they say very little about the actual process of collecting and compiling. They can be compared with haiku poems whereby very little is said, but what is not said is as important as what is said. If we read colonial texts on method of collecting folklore like haiku texts, we will notice what is not said, and this will put what is said in a new perspective. Some of the factors which are rarely mentioned are the following:

- The exact place(s) of collection.
- The person(s) who actually wrote from hearing the narrator(s).
- The language in which that first text was written and what happened to that text.
- The when, where, and how of the translation processes and the exact role of native assistants therein.
- Any future plan of preservation and promotion of performative folklores that were observed, documented, and described as "under pressure of modernity."
- Any effort toward institutionalization of folklore studies in the colonies and building infrastructure toward its research. (Given the bureaucratic powers of the collectors, it seems that they would have been able to at least initiate

building of institutions and infrastructure, but the expression of any such intent on the part of the colonial collectors is largely missing).

These factors rarely mentioned in the published works of colonial British folklore collectors have contributed by their absence toward a certain kind of historiography of colonial folkloristics. In this historiography the colonial collectors are either idolized as pioneers or demonized as colonizers. My concern is somewhat different in that I am trying not to reach final conclusions, but to form a reliable picture of the method of colonial folkloristics. The point I am making is that it is part of colonial method to maintain silence over these issues or to spare just a few words for them. As constant features of colonial writings, these silences also define the colonial folkloristics. The definition which emerges when we take these factors of absence into consideration is: colonial folkloristics was made with the intellectual labor of colonized peoples; this labor was assumed to be the right of the collector and thus was not thought to be notable or worth mentioning; and British colonial collectors were not concerned with the real conditions of the narrative and performative practices with which they felt charmed and with which they successfully charmed their readers.

In the colonial folkloristic method the most important tasks of the accredited folklore collector were to select out of the available folklores, organize the collection of data, engage with translation process and texts, and see to their publication. These tasks depended on the collector's ability to exploit the given opportunities and to cull a record. The collector often did not understand this record in the original language, but understood it best in translation. Colonial method also did not require preservation and publication of manuscripts in local languages. Ethical transgressions were the norm in colonial folkloristics, and peaked in the silence over the exact role of the native assistants and associates.

It may be argued that the colonial British collectors did not see their practices as ethical transgressions, and many of their so-called "transgressions," such as not acknowledging the narrators, were also common practices in European folkloristics of the times. The Grimms did it! This is, however, not exactly comparable, because collectors like the Grimm brothers did feel, and legitimately so, that the folklore they were documenting was also their *own* heritage, and not only that of the narrators. Linguistically too they were in a position to do all the work of "translation" themselves. In the colonial contexts such imaginings, illusions, and delusions were not possible. British collectors knew very well that their planned and innovative methods could not fructify without the active engagement of native associates. Almost all the projects we have discussed got off the ground once the British collector had been able to identify one or more such associates. Therefore, silence over this and other such aspects could not be a matter of contemporary norms, but a conscious practice based on other factors. If we recall the motivations of the collectors at this point, we will notice that almost all of the collectors were trying to gain a distinctive identity for themselves back home. Their silence therefore seems not unconscious, but motivated by self-interest. Could Jacob Grimm publish without Wilhelm Grimm as co-author, or vice versa? Obviously not, but Richard Temple, Robert Rattray, William Crooke, and others could and did diminish the importance of Chaina Mull, Victor Aboya, and Ram Gharib Chaube to their respective collections by their full or partial silence about the extent of contribution by their respective native associates. The issue, therefore, is not ethical norms then and now, but systematic silences in the verbalization of the methods colonial collectors followed in the field. Method encapsulates the entirety of principles and strategies and not only the statement made by the collectors.

The word "official" has yet another meaning here: this method involved the use of official machinery in some form or another. The project to collect may or may not have been funded by the state, but the infrastructure and authority of the colonial state was involved in the method of folklore collection. This included the privileges of power, directly (for example, in the capacity to summon narrators to official residences and have them narrate in this artificial situation) and indirectly (for example, the intangible power of authority and its larger context).

In this complex set of circumstances colonial officials and missionaries compiled voluminous collections of folklore, including the performance of oral religious texts. Folklore specifically was both an independent area of interest and almost a necessary part of every anthropological project. The peak of this combination seems to have been reached in the case of Rattray, the collector of Hausa and Chinyanja folklore. He was recognized as a scholar by the academics in Oxford (Rattray 1913) and later—in the early 1920s—established a state-funded Department of Anthropology in Nigeria for the study of Ashanti, of which he was the sole custodian.

Rattray's final anthropological project, published in 1923, reflects the changing consciousness of colonial collectors with regard to the problems of communication faced by earlier collectors, including the way narrators were treated. "A standard conception of professionalizing anthropology between the wars was that, to avoid colonial struggle—race conflict, indigenous revolt—one should follow a colonial strategy based on anthropological knowledge and planning to achieve the desired evolutionary progress cheaply and without bloodshed" (Pels 1997, 164). This comment applies to Rattray and his role in the famous "golden stool controversy" among the Ashanti in present-day Ghana. The Ashanti people, themselves rulers of a great Empire, were the last to lose their sovereignty to the British in Africa. They had been militarily subjugated in 1900, and in the following two decades the loss and finding of their spiritual and political symbol—a golden stool—created unrest that threatened the colonial rule in that country. Rattray's advice was sought and accepted, and it helped to pacify the angry people. Subsequently he was appointed "Government Anthropologist," which enabled him to conduct extensive researches among the Ashanti (Machin 1998). Rattray's extensive knowledge, gained over decades, enabled him to imagine a situation in which the problems of communication may be circumvented: "If, however, they are able to talk freely and without the aid of an interpreter to one who has their confidence, who they know can sympathize with them and understand not only their language, but their modes of thought and pride of race, then and then only are they likely to pour out their store of ancient lore and to lay bare their thoughts" (Rattray 1923, 7). Having considered the possibility and himself possessing the required skills, he took the following course of action: "I approached these old people and this difficult subject [their religious beliefs] in the spirit of one who came to them as a seeker after truths, the key to which I told them they alone possessed, which not all the learning nor all the books of the white man could ever give to me. I made it clear to them that I asked access to their religious rites such as are herein described for this reason" (Rattray 1923, 11).

This much explanation was, however, not all the explaining he apparently did, and the same text details lengthy conversations, and although Rattray appears to be offering the explanations on his own, yet it can and should be assumed that at least some of these were responses to direct questions from the other side, while indirect pressure and/or resistance demanded some. Clearly, Rattray's defensive tone also derives from the cautious approach after the "golden stool" episode.

The silence of the "colonized" is not an exclusive feature of the colonial folklore scholarship, but runs through the entire gamut of literature implied under Said's concept of "Orientalism." In folklore studies it gains yet another dimension: the silence makes the text incomplete, actually halved, and we, the readers, are like people listening to one side of a telephone conversation and deducing half the dialogue. Rattray lists a number of clarifications and explanations he offered to his subjects, some of which are quoted below. It is also noteworthy that there is a twentieth-century consciousness emerging wherein the native's consent is being sought, or at least it is necessary to point out to the European readers that the natives were informed about the purposes of research. This is not a feature of early colonial folklore scholarship. However, Rattray's perception of informed consent belongs to the colonial world:

> *I have told them that the work of the new Department is to study their institutions, which the rising generation is tempted to despise. . . . I have tried to make the people understand that we are here among them to help them* by grafting on to their institutions such of our own *as will enable them to take their place in the commonwealth of civilized nations, not as denationalised Ashanti, but as an African People who will become the greater force and power in the Empire because they have not bartered the wealth of their past, metaphorically and not infrequently in reality, for a coat, a collar, or a tie. The response to* this appeal, which was my apologia for prying into their secrets, *the genuine understanding, the gratitude and the wish for a helping hand to assist them over this critical stage of their evolution. . . . (Rattray 1923, 12, emphasis added)*

These excerpts from a far lengthier text highlight the essential nature of colonial folklore collections. The dividing lines between the narrator and the collectors were not of class, as they clearly belonged to two different systems of social beliefs. Instead, they were historically in a new system of hierarchy: the collector represented the power of the state for the narrator, and the narrator represented above all the colonized subject who was obliged to communicate what he was being asked. The atmosphere seems to have been largely of mistrust on either side: the collector not sure whether he was getting the genuine and complete stuff, and the narrator suspicious of the purpose of recording. Added to this was the mutual linguistic ignorance and cultural otherness.

However, if we consider both the mistrust and the ignorance, and the measures adopted to textualize orality, we will see the meaning of these processes for the discipline of folkloristics. Having seen that all these features are rooted in the colonial context, let us focus only on the process of textualization of orality. In this image are visible collectors faced with circumstances beyond the imagination of their colleagues collecting folklore within the region of their birth, nationality, and language. The experiences, ideals, and theories of their European colleagues cannot help them much, as they fall short of the complexities of reality. The challenges of this wide variety of situations compel them to imagine and invent methods. Their methods seem on the surface like simple solutions to complex problems, but they are more than functional tools. Their methods are their contribution to the field of folkloristics. The field of folklore research was crystallizing itself as an international and intercultural field of study, and the features of colonial folkloristics would be reflected in folklore theory, methods of collection, and classification for a long time to come. Indeed, until today, classification systems based on indigenous categories of South Asian and African folklore have seldom been developed. This was one side of the coin.

The other side of the coin was the popularization of the European concept of folklore among the colonized. Between the collector and the narrator were local people who were crucial to the success of communication. They were there in the role of assistant or associate of the collector. They were also there in the role of the patrons of the narrators. They were often there simply as witnesses to the act of documentation of orality. Each of these persons influenced the process of textualization, but they were also influenced by the process. Their oral expressive cultures were gaining a new meaning, even a new currency. Narratives which had had purely ritualistic significance were transforming into representations of their practitioners. "Folklore" became a universal word, and so did the idea that it was "collectable," "displayable," and thereafter "representative" in nature.

The two sides of this same coin—development of the discipline of folkloristics through the search for methods and the induction of a European view of folklore across the world—have not remained without legacy. The erstwhile colonized world uses folklore in the construction of its national identities and still supplies ethnic entertainment to the former colonial powers. On the other hand, while folklorists from the former colonizing nations go to the previously colonized world to collect folklore, the reverse of this situation is still a rarity. Colonial folkloristics internationalized the discipline, but its "colonial" legacy was embedded in the inheritance of postcolonial folkloristics.

Part of this inheritance is that the "native assistant or associate" is acknowledged across the continents, tribes, and other communities, yet has no identity in the history of colonial folkloristics. How many different "natives" helped the British collectors to record, decode, and interpret the lore of their people may never be known, yet it would be a very conservative estimate to say that the native assistants outnumbered the British folklore collectors by at least three to one, and perhaps five to one. A far more difficult issue is determining the extent of their contribution, given the unique context of each collection. Mary Frere granted her narrator an autobiographical identity, and Frere herself was the one who recorded from the oral narration. For all other collectors the situation involved more than two persons and languages. Temple's assistant, Chaina Mull, created manuscripts in Persian which are available for study in the India Office and Records Library (British Library, European Manuscripts, Eur Mss F98), but Chaina Mull is not even a known name in the history of Indian folkloristics. In most of the collections from the British Empire the native assistants and associates remain anonymous or just names without personalities. Individual identities belong only to the British colonial collectors. Their own claims have been the basis of the history of folkloristics.

Genealogies, like that of Richard Dorson (1968), construct the narrative on colonial folklore collectors and collections as a fantastic adventure and safari in which the collector emerges heroic in stature. Largely, the colonial British collectors created this image, which was believed in by their contemporaries and institutionalized by the colonial state in the form of grant of awards, academic recognition, and institutional infrastructure in Britain.

The evident fact is that it was not the collector who knew the two languages well, but the assistant who knew two or more languages and also understood the oral narrative or song beyond its linguistic meaning. As is evident, most narrators could not have established a direct communication with the British collector, even if they narrated for weeks sitting in front of him. The man who would finally communicate their text to the British collector was the assistant. The acknowledgments of the British collectors point to a wide variety of people who assisted them, and we will discuss some of the innovative ways of using natives in colonial folklore collection in a later section of this chapter called "Native Folklorists of Colonial Archives." At this point here we are talking about the so-called "native assistant" who accompanied the British folklore collector wherever the collection was made, that is, he was present on the spot. He was part of the method devised by the British collector. He often took down the first written record of the oral text, in the language of narration. Simultaneously he established communication between the collector and the narrators at two planes—linguistic and interpretative—by "communicating" the wishes and responses of either side. After the recording he helped the collector understand the texts, most often translating them either into another local language that the collector knew, sometimes helping create the English translations, and not infrequently translating the texts into English—most often "refined" by the collector before publication. In spite of the varied capacities of "assistants" across colonies with different intellectual traditions, these were some of the basic and common functions performed by the assistants. It is important to note that this fact points to the availability of men with knowledge of the English language, even though their capacities varied, across the colonial Empire. Seen from the point of view of the modern intellectual histories of the colonies, this is an important development, which started determining linguistic politics, policies, and social transformation in those countries—a process discussed by postcolonial Indian theorist Dipesh Chakraborty in his work *Provincializing Europe* (2000).

The involvement of the native assistants also points to the transference of the knowledge of the discipline of folkloristics. Within the intellectual histories of their nation they were playing the role of objectifying tradition as something separate from rules governing living. Silence on their role is an equally universal phenomenon of colonial folkloristics, and that includes an even deadlier silence on their motivations and strategies of intercultural communication. It seems unlikely that we will ever know a systematic story of even one assistant. We may at best be able to decipher fragments of the contributions of a few of them across countries and cultures in Asia and Africa. These fragments may give us only an impression of the larger picture, but even that would be of considerable significance toward our understanding of colonial folkloristics. This, however, requires detailed study of individual locales, their intellectual histories, and therein the place of people who became assistants to British collectors and the trajectories of their personal lives.[5] Tracing the roles of native assistants across the British Empire is beyond the scope of the present work and, presumably, beyond the capacities of any individual scholar. Such a work could emerge through collaborative research by folklorists from different countries.

The point here is that the relationship between the collector and his assistant or assistants represents a very crucial aspect of the colonial folkloristic *method*—one that takes us away from the stereotypical versions of colonial writers and postcolonial genealogies—and gives a sense of the real methods of folklore collection in the colonies. Some common and some unique aspects of this relationship are reflected in the case of British civil servant and renowned anthropologist and folklorist William Crooke (1848–1923) and his Indian associate Pandit Ram Gharib Chaube (?–1914). Crooke's entire collection of north Indian folktales is in the handwriting of Chaube, who translated the texts from many dialects of Hindi language and rendered them in English language texts along with notes on narrators and narratives, on signs and symbols, and on the meaning of the narratives.

Crooke and Chaube's collection of folktales of northern India (Naithani 2002a, 2006a) is still today the largest scientific collection of Indian folktales and one of the largest colonial projects. Chaube's emergence as the main creator of the written texts shows extensively the role of native associates. Crooke and Chaube's case points to the need for an evaluation and placement of native assistants. The colonial folklore collections were not born of individual scholarship but of teamwork, and it was created by the intellectual labor of people on both sides of the colonial divide.

Method in colonial folkloristics was intercultural in perception, multilingual in the process, and multinational in its spread and influence. It cannot be defined by national identifications like "Indian" or "Nigerian." The term "British" that has been in use has erased the multiple agencies in the creation of colonial collections. Terms like Indo-British or Afro-British are applicable to only parts of it, but not to the whole. The whole requires a term because it was perceived and experienced as whole in the center of the Empire. "Colonial Folkloristics" is a term that defines it with reference to historical time, ideological stance, and political implications.

THE AMAZING METHOD

A few sporadic records of orality follow no designated method, nor do they attempt to prove the authenticity of their record. These find no mention in the regular genealogies of colonial folklore collections. What sets them apart is that their authors came across the stories in an unpredictable manner and invented a method spontaneously to reach more stories. In their individual ways they attempted to break barriers of communication by personal engagement. For that reason their methods and compilations cannot be compared with other collections, nor be evaluated on a general scale. They require individual attention. The adjective "amazing" is not only my postcolonial comment. The authors and their audience were aware of this characteristic, as will be evident in the following examples. These texts are included for analysis in this volume because by providing a contrast they illuminate many aspects of the standard method that otherwise remain obscured. For example, they lead to newer insights into the mind of the collector—a factor that colors all colonial writings but itself remains colorless. The official method always sought to explain and justify itself as scientific, but the amazing method was presented unabashed, and was intended to attract the common readers. Amazing methods show us glimpses of the colonizers' minds, even if they do not produce dependable folklore collections. In certain instances, like that of Frank Hives, the amazing methods also lead to different kinds of narratives being recorded, not necessarily those identified with a particular form of performance. They also show aspects of intercultural communications outside the boundaries of a formal event of recording.

The adjective "amazing" is also applied here to methods of colonial collectors in Australia, where the native populace had been considerably decimated before folklore collectors appeared. The methods followed by colonial officials and visiting scholars had almost nothing in common with the "standard" method of their colleagues in South Asia and Africa.

Entering the Sphere of the Other

One of the "amazing" methods was that the folklore collector changed his identity. There are two interesting instances of this, the second of which we will discuss in greater detail. The first one is brief, but illustrative. A military officer, Captain C. F. Mackenzie, adopted a pen name, "Il Musannif"—literally, the composer—to publish the tales he had collected. What's in a name? one might ask, in a manner of speaking. Indeed, there is a lot in a name: it evokes the regional, religious, and linguistic identity of the author, and the associations and expectations of the reader. It implies in this context a relationship between the narratives and the collector that is not factual. The change of name here seeks to erase the otherness of the collector to the narratives.

Rev. Weeks, author of *Congo Life and Folklore*, did not change just his name, but his entire being—he imagined himself to be a *brass rod*! Why a brass rod of all things in the world? He had seen in Congo that "A Brass rod is the money of by far the larger number of the people on the Lower and Upper Congo. In thickness it is not quite so stout as an ordinary slate pencil, and varies now in length, according to the tribe using it, from five inches long on the Lower Congo to an indefinite length among the more distant tribes of Congo's hinterland" (Weeks 1911, vii). He also saw that a piece of brass rod changed hands several time and was "worn first around the neck of one owner and then around the arm of another" (ibid., ix). Since "For a considerable time" he had been "interested in the folklore and anthropology of the people, and [had] made long and careful notes on such subjects," he decided to write "under the guise of a Brass Rod" (ibid., viii) that remains with the natives even at times when the foreigner cannot observe them or hear their conversation with other natives. Rev. Weeks first imagined himself to be a brass rod and then claimed to have had the vantage point of observation. He wrote about it as if a brass rod was cognizant of human realities. "By writing under the guise of a Brass Rod, worn first around the neck of one owner and then around the arm of another, the writer has had more scope, and hopes he has been able to make the scenes from life more realistic than he could have done by the ordinary method" (ibid., ix). So, as a brass rod Weeks was more concerned with the "people of the country [Congo]—their habits, customs, views of life and superstitions—than with the scenery." And with this book Weeks wanted "to lay clearly before the reader the ingrained prejudices, the curious views, the tremendous and all-pervading superstitions, and the mighty forces that have been arrayed against the introduction of Christianity into that benighted land . . ." (Weeks 1911, ix).

From the folklore he had gathered "some of this information he . . . worked into the story" (ibid., viii). And although the life of a brass rod was only a fantasy, yet Weeks claimed "that which finds a place in the following pages can be accepted as perfectly trustworthy and true to Congo life" (ibid., viii). The contents of his book, he said, were not only trustworthy but even "the views and prejudices of the natives are faithfully pourtrayed [*sic*] and are not exaggerated . . ." (ibid., viii–ix).

What is amazing is how Weeks mixes up his imagination with the reality of life of the people of Congo. He tells you that it is an imagined text and then demands trust in the texts and in him as a writer. And already in the introduction he tells us where the investigations have led him: "The missionary and other experiences are found on fact, . . . and the native superstitions have, as shown here, resulted in innumerable cases of murder by ordeal . . ." (ibid., viii–ix). The method employed by Weeks was amazing as it reveals the mind of the writer more than that of the subject. The wish for as intimate a view of the native life as possible; seeing himself as the currency for natives; imagining being an invisible witness to in-group discourses. And yet it was only imagination. Weeks could not have been a brass rod worn around the neck of a native, but the fantasy gives him the legitimacy to represent the in-group discourse of the natives, including what they think of the white rulers. How legitimate and realistic this "figment" of Weeks's imagination is—that is not the question we are seeking to answer through this analysis. The fact remains that faced with the same problems as other contemporary folklore collectors—to be able to view the native life without being simultaneously observed, to reveal the secrets of the native and to know how the white rule was being perceived—Weeks hit upon a novel trope.

Weeks's text also points to another aspect of colonial writings, their story-like nature. We noted earlier that the image of the folklore collector was that of a folkloristic hero and his successful adventures. This is an aspect often not highlighted in the writings, but clearly articulated in some of the texts wherein the writers consciously wrote it as a story. Weeks is a good example of this.

Collecting Simply

Alice Elizabeth Dracott, the wife of a British civil servant in India, produced two collections of folktales. The first, *Folktales from Central India* (1896), a small booklet, is a case in point here. Dracott decided not to imagine herself as somebody else that she was not, but to imagine and present herself as she was and the place of stories in her life. Her booklet is without a preface/introduction/interpretation by the collector. It opens in an unassuming manner and its pattern resembles an ordinary day in the life of a British housewife in colonial India. "'Belaitee' stood under the shadow of the purple *impomea* creeper in the verandah of my little bungalow at Goona, and made a picturesque enough figure in his flowing dress and big Punjabi turban. He had arrived at an opportune moment, just as 'Ramchand' the *Ooloo* had finished telling me a tale, so he added his comments . . ." (Dracott 1896, 1).[6]

Flanked by domestic servants for any need from dawn to midnight, the British Mem Sahibs's major amount of time was spent in the company of these people. Closeness, friendliness, and generosity is visible and she regularly uses their nicknames. In Dracott's book these people transform into storytellers, as they narrate stories to her in the course of the daily chores or as they comment on each other. She has reproduced this structure of narration in her booklet. The absence of preface or introduction shows that the method had probably been used unconsciously, and not as an extra attempt, like that of Weeks, to search for a new form. Yet this little booklet brings out a world of people and their stories. Dracott does not pretend to hide her difference of race, class, and attitude. Her method is amazing because she is able to see and portray the narrative situation in a household with British masters/employers and Indian domestic servants. Instead of creating a formal and artificial situation of narration, she seems to use the familiarity with her narrators as a reason for their telling her stories voluntarily and so records the narratives she hears in the course of daily conversation between herself and the servants and among the latter themselves. She tells us that her knowledge of Hindustani is what any "subaltern" would have, that is, she would have known the functional language for daily needs. She therefore would have been able to ask questions that led to the narratives we have in the book, and she would have been able to understand simple narratives with probably a few words of English thrown in by the narrators. The superiority and imposing nature of her position, thus softened by daily contact, brings forth more than a collection of narratives; it shows glimpses of a new situation of storytelling and a new set of narrators—to this I shall return later in this discussion on amazing methods.

Dracott's folktale collection becomes a glimpse of a new situation of narration and a new set of narrators created within the context of colonial rule across the Empire in Asia and Africa. This is the situation where the collectors are in a certain kind of social relationship with the narrators, most commonly as employers of domestic servants. This situation and the narrators need consideration to determine how they are unique in themselves. The common characteristics of this group of narrators and their situation are that they came from the lower, most often rural, strata of the colony concerned, they were illiterate, and they performed various domestic tasks, from cleaning to cooking to looking after the children of the employers. They were thus exposed to the European ways of living, their employers' likes and dislikes, and had learned to perform their roles accordingly. Most of them had picked up enough English to understand commands and wishes and to communicate responses. This knowledge depended on the specific nature of the job and the interaction it required with the employers. Looking after children generated the maximum knowledge of English, while ironing clothes required minimal verbal communication. They, like their employers, were living in a multilingual situation where their personal lives were governed by their mother tongue. Mary Frere's ayah, Anna Liberata de Souza, notwithstanding her primary level education, fluency in English, and religion, seems like the identifiable epitome of this group of narrators. Dracott has a whole array of them lined up for entertainment. And there would be many more such narrators across the colonial Empire, even though the specifics of their service may have been different. Neither they as a group nor their situation of storytelling can be defined with reference to tradition, community, and other ethnic identities. This is not to say that their narratives did not have a tradition, nor that they as individuals did not belong to a community, but to say that as narrators we find them in a situation whereby they themselves and the situation need to be defined by other terms as well in order to be defined correctly. The social-psychological complexity of the situation needs to be explored, because it concerns narration, reception, and documentation of oral narratives.

Mixing Natural and Supernatural Spheres

The opposite of Dracott's domestic life was that of Frank Hives, who narrated many interesting records from different colonies—Australia, Africa, Jamaica—concerning his experiences of a supernatural kind. His friend Gascoigne Lumley decided to retell the "tales" because "*They are true stories of things that happened and of people he [Hives] knew*" (Hives 1930, v). What makes them interesting and relevant for folkloristics is that many of these stories are records of real events in which narratives, traditional and contemporary, play an important role. These narratives would themselves be subjects of folklore, but their being represented as part of real-life events adds another dimension to our discussion on colonialism and folklore. Real-life matters were communicated across the cultural boundaries to influence colonial rule, and these events themselves become "stories" when narrated, initially orally, by Hives to his compatriot and colleague, Lumley. To understand the significance of Hives's stories, it is necessary to know the story of his life, too. Lumley introduces him:

> *Hives belongs to a former generation of administrators, and was in his younger days essentially a pioneer. When he first went to Nigeria the hinterland of that protectorate was hardly touched by the civilizing influences of Trade and Government, which were confined to a few stations on the coast and on the banks of the Niger. But the country had to be opened up; and for this task were needed men possessing the qualities of resourcefulness, courage and common sense rather than mere ability to pass examinations. Hives was endowed with these qualities in no small measure . . . (Hives and Lumley 1930, v)*

Hives's capabilities were not merely instinctive, but based on experience in another locale of the Empire. Hives' career points to connectivity of colonial rule not only as a system, but in terms of the movement of people—at this stage, that of the British residents between different colonies. This implies similarities in ways of doing things in different locales, and applies to methods of folklore collection as well. Lumley again enlightens us about Hives:

> *. . . he did not go to Nigeria without previous experience. For nearly seventeen years he had roughed it in North Queensland and other Colonies. He was therefore accustomed to life in the wilds. . . . His knowledge of "bushwhacking" was invaluable, and it was utilized to the full by those who had the ordering of his career. For whenever there was a difficult or dangerous*

undertaking, such as the opening of a new station, the pacification of a rebellious one, or a political adviser needed for an expedition, he was the man to be selected. Some of his tales are incidents that happened on such occasions. (Hives and Lumley 1930, v–vi)

Lumley thus establishes the connection between Hives's professional world and the narratives—as stories coming from a man moving amid different people in unknown locales. As the volume was co-authored, in his introduction Hives pre-empts the question regarding the authenticity of details and whether he might have forgotten parts of the narratives that he did not write down when he heard or experienced them. He says, "The native is given to exaggerating, so I expect the tale my followers told lost nothing in the telling" (ibid., 84). The logic is a bit convoluted and needs explanation: since the natives exaggerate so much, no matter how much one forgets in the retelling of the stories, the narrative would still come through. The collector's memory seems to have been a sieve from which only the exaggerations would drain out, and the narrative would remain.

One of the narratives related by Hives is called "The Rest House" (ibid., 85). On this occasion Hives had marched with three natives through the day to reach a place where some British soldiers had built a rest house a couple of years previous to his visit, but the place had not been visited by any official since then. On reaching there and through the evening he noticed the natives to be behaving peculiarly and ultimately got the hint that the rest house was haunted. Obviously, the enlightened white man could not have given in to such superstitious ways of living. He got his bed placed on the verandah, sent the servants to their rooms, and decided to sleep. But that was not to last long, as he was woken up by a sound, and on waking up found that the chair had moved from its position, and before he could understand it he saw the table move without anyone's assistance and without making any marks on the sand on the floor. The verandah was simultaneously filling up with an unbearable stench.

He took out his pistol and looked around in the dark:

The first thing I saw was what I took to be the head of a very old native. Then the rest of the body appeared, crawling very slowly on hands and knees and not making a sound. Presently the creature came within the radius of the lamplight so that I could see it more clearly. A more horrible sight I have never seen, a more loathsome thing I hope never to see. The face was mottled with pock marks and the nose had been eaten away. The head was

> bald, the top of it being a dirty white, while the rest of the body was like old and mouldy leather, shriveled and grey in patches. And the eyes—oh, those dreadful eyes. Never shall I forget them, as the head turned towards me. They were without life or expression, just two staring, dead eyes that did not move. The horrible, lipless mouth was half open, the jaw sagging like that of a dead person.
> Slowly and silently it crawled across the sanded veranda. It was quite naked, and in one hand appeared to be holding a native-made rope, which it dragged after it as it moved. (ibid., 97)

The experience was dramatic and puzzling. Hives's rational mind could not understand what to make of this event, and he says:

> I determined to find out what I could about the history of the place. But I knew it would be of no use sending for the chiefs; they would, like all primitive peoples, tell as little as possible to a white man. So I sent the interpreter to the town with orders to find, if he could, an intelligent native.
> After a while he returned with a bright-looking youth, dressed in khaki shorts and shirt . . . Benjamin Oku . . . educated at the Calabar mission . . . [a] clerk employed by one of the trading firms in Calabar. (ibid., 98–99, emphasis added)

After being cajoled, the boy Benjamin Oku decided to tell what everyone except Hives knew, but not before excusing himself by disowning the story for himself, and secondly, making Hives agree that he would not tell anyone that he (the boy) told him the story. Benjamin—educated at the mission, converted to Christianity, and earning his living as a clerk in an English trading organization—knew that he was caught between two world-views, something which his grandfathers probably never experienced. He was part of both systems and, walking the tightrope, he communicated to Hives the popular lore, beginning with the history of the rest house. Long before the white men came to the place, the ground on which the rest house had "been built was the ju-ju sacrificial grove" (ibid., 99). Hives continued to tell the story to Lumley:

> About two years before my visit troops had "halted" for some weeks at Isuingu, and the white man in command had ordered the people to build a rest house, choosing as the site the ju-ju ground. And although the chiefs and various others of the people had suggested other and better sites, he had been

adamant—doubtless thinking this the best way to stamp out entirely the superstitious and savage customs the place stood for. The old ju-ju priest had evidently become crazy when he saw what was happening to his preserves, and lodged a violent protest. But the white man's reply to this had been to make him assist at the demolition of the grove. The same evening he had cast spells—cursing the place, and swearing that no white man should ever rest in peace in the house that was to be built on what, to him, was sacred ground. The chiefs and people had been terrified at these curses, but in spite of this they were obliged to build the house, and on the day it was finished the troops departed.

On the day after that the old priest was seen wandering round the house, repeating his spells and wailing loudly. The following morning his dead body was seen hanging from the main ridge-pole of the house, in the passage between the two rooms. He had evidently climbed up from the inside of the roof, an extraordinary feat for such an old man, and hanged himself with a piece of native rope.

The people had been too frightened to cut the body down; so it had hung there until it rotted. Then it had fallen piece-meal to the ground and been "cleaned up" by the scavenger pigs of the town, so that nothing remained. (ibid., 99–100)

Benjamin's description of the former priest matched with the "apparition." Hives then suggested to the chiefs, on some other pretext, that he would like to change the place of the rest house. The suggestion was very welcome, as he says, and they helped him to find the best locale for the new rest house. This was quickly made with local labor, and Hives torched the old one. Hives closed his narration by saying that he has slept many peaceful nights in the new rest house. But did he believe in ghosts thereafter? "What was it I saw that night? An elemental? The earth-bound spirit of the old priest praying for the crimes he had committed during his life? And how to account for the horrible and indescribable stench that pervaded the house when the apparition was 'appearing'? I cannot" (ibid., 102).

Hives's story has layers of narratives within it: the narratives surrounding the ju-ju worship before the British came, the narratives about the powers of the priests, the colonial official narratives about human sacrifices in ju-ju temples and the banning of the ju-ju worship, the narratives around the destruction of this particular ju-ju locale, the fate of its priest, who had a completely different position before the colonial rule, the witnessing of his humiliation by the locals who presumably would have been in awe of him earlier, the debasement of the authority of the local chiefs, the establishment of Christianity and of colonial administration. All these narratives get entangled in one another in real history and culminate into one record of it—the story by Hives. Indeed, it is an important record not for its direct references, but for the violence involved in the displacement of existing narratives, their resilience and survival, and the establishment of new narratives reflected in it. Popular beliefs and associated narratives are documented here as Hives confronted them in the course of his life in Nigeria. Reality merges into narrative and narrative determines reality. In the story of the rest house, there is a sub-text, visible with little effort. Ju-Ju worship was an important institution of religious and judicial nature. Its practice involved social organization that accepted it as a governing system. If it had been only a religious system, it may have been allowed to survive in the margins, but as a system of justice it interfered with the administrative functioning of the state, which could not have allowed a parallel system of justice. In a circular argument, however, it was based on a system of faith that could not be erased by erasing the institution alone. The authority of the ju-ju priests now competed with the authority of colonial administrators and the state. In the above quoted story, Hives's predecessor had not ordered the demolition of the ju-ju temple and the construction of the rest house on the same spot just like that. Each of those acts had a symbolic meaning—the displacement of the former institutional and spiritual authority by a new one. The explanation told to Hives by the boy Benjamin evidences the resentment of the locals, even though they had been unable to oppose the foreigners tooth and nail. All these factors suggest another possible layer to the ghost episode—did someone alive consciously try to influence Hives into changing the locale of the rest house?[7] One may also ask whether Hives's response to the situation shows a pragmatic approach whereby he knew that the rest house had served the function of displacing the temple or whether it reflects a psychological state born of guilt, foreignness, and real threats.

Hives's method constitutes one of the most interesting narratives of its kind and is related to storytelling in the colonial context. Interestingly, ghost stories were narrated in other locales of the Empire as well.

In the 1880s two "ghost stories" influenced public life in northern India. "Momia wala Sahib" and "Dinapur wala Sahib"—two stories that depicted white gentlemen as ghosts, armed with contracts from the government for their different purposes: kidnapping native boys and extracting juices from their bodies to make medicine; and chopping off the heads of natives with a pair of shears and sending them to a museum in England, respectively

(Crooke 1892, 177–79). The motivations, locales (hill stations, cantonment areas), and international operations of these ghosts were so linked with colonial institutions that their symbolic value and messages cannot be ignored. Moreover, their narration instigated the populace to link living British officials with the images and stir unrest. Many other British officers from the Indian subcontinent reported that their staff narrated stories of ghosts of their British predecessors haunting the concerned office or residence (Naithani 2006b, 139–50).

The spread of ghost stories and their use in real-time communication with the colonial rulers point at one level to the emergence of new folklore, and at another, to a new role that folklore in the colonies was adapting itself to. With the tools of oral storytelling new narratives were being created for new effects. These stories also point to the fact that we know very little about the way colonialism influenced folklore itself in the colonies. What we do know and discuss are sociological changes brought into the life of narrators influencing the present and future existence of traditional folklore. We know very little how this phase of cultural contact and confrontation between peoples got reflected in the oral lore of the colonized peoples. Such subjects did not constitute a category of folklore for colonial collectors for limitations of knowledge and reasons of politics. Such material has also not been a subject of research for postcolonial scholars, and the blank emphasizes the fact that studies of folklore of the erstwhile colonized world are still defined by the parameters, subject areas, and narrative communities identified by the colonial collectors. We would probably also need "amazing" methods to be able to reach this alternative material.

Creating the Exterminated

In Australia, any method should be considered "amazing," because of the degree to which the native populace had been annihilated by the colonizers. Bonwick's introductory sentence to his collection of folklore reports the irony: "The departed race once lived and laughed in the world" (Bonwick 1870, 1). The "race" of people who lived there had already "departed" by 1870. And in 1879 Rev. Taplin was reporting this: "In the following pages there will be seen to exist a deficiency of information concerning the Adelaide tribe. Every effort was made to obtain a knowledge of the manners and customs of this people, but without success. Almost nothing is left in the records of the Aborigines' Department about their folklore, superstitions, or language. Probably papers have unwittingly been destroyed which contained such information" (Taplin

1879, vii). Taplin gave the statistics of 1861—surviving aborigines: 3,780. And these were living in depots and camps; in other words, they were captured and removed from their way of life already. Taplin's record was drawn with the help of the governor's approval, which had come following a suggestion from Dr. Immanuel Bleek, the renowned collector of South African folklore, that similar records should be made of the Australian aborigines. To facilitate Taplin's research, a circular containing questions was sent to "keepers of aborigines' depots throughout the colony" (ibid., vii), and to the institution which helped in drawing up the record: "The police of the colony rendered very efficient help. It will be seen that some interesting replies came from intelligent and observant troopers" (ibid., viii). The information did not come directly from the native people, but from their captors! This is indeed a morbid source of oral narratives, probably unparalleled in history. In spite of the extremity of the situation, the missionary Taplin offered the book "to those who seek for truth respecting the human race, and who would gather up every contribution which may cast light upon the natural history of mankind" (ibid., viii).

An amateur collector, Mrs. K. Langloh Parker managed to collect from the natives, as she was a resident herself. In 1898, she published her second book, *More Australian Legends*: "The present series of legends have all been collected by myself from the Blacks, as were the previous ones" (ibid., ix). She asked Andrew Lang to write an introduction, and he obliged, commenting on her narrators: "These dark backward friends of hers, 'the blacks'... are our superiors in poetical fancy. Without our savage ancestors we should certainly have had no poetry" (ibid., xvii). For Lang, the Australians were "just escaping from the Paleolithic age" (ibid., xviii). He saw in the stories confirmation of his own thesis: "this helps my argument (that theism is not the latest flower of animism) very well.... I have maintained... that religion and mythology represent quite different moods of men" (ibid., xxi–xxii).

The 1923 address of the president of the Folk-Lore Society, Henry Balfour, was titled "The Welfare of Primitive Peoples." The speaker was mainly concerned with the Naga tribes in the eastern part of India, but drew his lesson from the British experience in Australia. "The past history of the effects of the contact of indigenous savage population with exotic civilized invaders, is not reassuring and give little ground for complacency. The extermination of the Tasmanians, one of the greatest blots upon the record of our colonial enterprise was a direct result of the advent of the White man.... Little or no attempt was officially made to study and to understand the natives and their 'point of view,' and but feeble and quite ineffectual effort was made to prevent their dying out" (Balfour 1923, 13–14). The British folklorists were aware of the harm caused by concepts like "primitive" and "savage," but could not find other words to replace them. Balfour was trying to avert the tragedy in other locales.

Writing in 1938, Professor A. P. Elkin said, "Interest in the Australian Aborigines as human personalities has increased during the past few years, and nowadays there is a growing desire not only to treat them justly, but also to help them rise culturally—if only we knew how" (Elkin 1938, v). If this realization was only a few years old in 1938, then it was already "too late" to "know" how their lot could be bettered. None of the attempts made by individuals could bring back the people, and Bonwick began his story, "The departed race once lived and laughed in the world." His aim was to tell "what they ate and how they built—what they sang and how they danced—what they thought and how they married—what were their ills and how they were buried—is the object of the present work." He continued narrating: "There was a time when no thought of the Whites disturbed the rude joys of the Island Barbarians. They lived as others had done before them" (Bonwick 1870, 1, 2). The absence of people themselves did not stop Bonwick from theorizing about them as savages "who knew no past, they wanted no future" and concluding, "They were true conservatives, and not only condemned innovation, but crushed it" (ibid., 1).

Information could be gained directly from the "natives" by the settlers or those whites who had put up farms and started to live there. They had captured natives to work on their farms. A second generation settler, Miss Parker described the location of her settlement with reference to "the nearest missionary settlement." She says that this "was founded after we settled among the Euahlayi.... None of my native informants had been at any time, to my knowledge, under the influence of missionaries" (Parker 1905, 2). Her informants had not been converted, but "They all wore shirts, and almost all of them trousers, on occasion; and all, except the old men, my chief sources, were employed by white settlers" (ibid.). So signs of western influence were visible, but not necessarily initiated by the missionaries, and natives had retained their faiths. The next question is about the language. Did the natives speak English or did the settlers speak the language of the native? Parker tells us:

> We conversed in a kind of lingua franca. An informant, say Peter, would try to express himself in English, when he thought that I was not successful in following him in his own tongue. With Paddy, who had no English,

> but a curse, I used two native women, one old, one younger, as interpreters, checking each other alternately. The younger natives themselves had lost the sense of some of the native words used by their elders, but the middle-aged interpreters were usually adequate. Occasionally there were disputes on linguistic points, when Paddt, a man already grey in 1845, would march off the scene, and need to be reconciled. They were on very good terms with me. (Parker 1905, 3)

In this account the collector had known the narrators since her childhood as workers on her father's farm, and knew the language of the natives. Obviously, she knew "her" language, English, too, and perhaps better, but the younger generation of the natives were dispossessed of the language of their ancestors. Disjunctions between language, culture, and country were all but complete for them: performance had disappeared from the country; text was disconnected from performative context; and narrator was disconnected from an audience that could understand the narrative. Actually, disjunction defined even Miss Parker, who was also living between the two worlds. Miss Parker's closeness to the natives was extreme as compared to other compilers. It is imaginable what it would have been like when folklore collections were made through police records.

The point, however, is that in the colonial context methods of folklore collection marched in the footsteps of the methods of colonization. The British folklore collectors did not ever challenge colonization and colonialism. Their interest in the folklores of the colonized subjects had clear boundaries of loyalty to their own race and nation.

NATIVE FOLKLORISTS OF COLONIAL ARCHIVES

In this section we will discuss the "native" folklorists. Our subjects are not the independent and nationalist folklorists in the colonies, or those that saw the collection of folklore as part of their fight against colonial rule—like the Finnish folklorist Elias Lonrott (Honko 1996), who has the status of national hero in his free country. We will be discussing here those that did produce independent works of folklore, but in close association with British folklore collectors, officials, missionaries, or women. Their independent productions differentiate them from native assistants and demand separate consideration. In this section we will also include works produced by natives on the insistence of a British collector.

Rev. Lal Behari Day was an Indian/Bengali missionary who authored *Folk-Tales of Bengal* in 1883 (reprint 1912?). This was his second work, the first being *Peasant Life in Bengal*.[8] Day's second work is intimately connected with this first book, which was a work of fiction. The title of the work does not suggest a fiction, because through "fiction" he was attempting to create a real-life image. In this book he created a "peasant boy Govinda" who spends "some hours every evening in listening to stories told by an old woman, who was called Sambhu's mother, and who was the best story-teller in the village" (Day 1912, vii). Day tells us, "On reading that passage, Captain R. C. Temple, of the Bengal Staff Corps, son of the distinguished Indian administrator Sir Richard Temple, wrote to me to say how interesting it would be to get a collection of those unwritten stories which old women in India recite to little children in the evenings, and to ask whether I could not make such a collection" (ibid.).

The connection between the colonial British and the native folklore collector is direct but mediated through another publication. Captain Temple was already renowned for his collections with Steel, and independently. His asking Day has many dimensions, but for the present I will concentrate on Day's perception of himself and his work. He is clearly implying above that he was important in the eyes of important British collectors. He substantiates it by listing his own qualifications: "As I was no stranger to the *Mährchen* [sic] of the Brothers Grimm, to the *Norse Tales* so admirably told by Dasent, to Arnason's *Icelandic Stories* translated by Powell, to the *Highland Stories* done into English by Campbell, and to the fairy stories collected by other writers . . ." (ibid., vii–viii). Day's qualifications point to the fact that contemporary European folklore scholarship was becoming known to a class of scholars in India, signifying another historical loop in folklore studies, the travel of European folkloristics to the colonies. This is a feature which would become an integral part of folkloristics in India and elsewhere. It is logical to assume that this would have influenced Day's selection and retelling of Bengali folktales. Accordingly, he saw a scholarly value to his work, that the collection would be a contribution "to that daily increasing literature of folklore and comparative mythology which, like comparative philosophy, proves that the swarthy and half-naked peasant on the banks of the Ganges is a cousin, albeit of the hundredth remove, to the fair-skinned and well-dressed Englishman on the banks of Thames" (viii). Apparently, Day was already under the influence of diffusionist theories. Temple's suggestion appealed to Day in every way, and he "readily caught up the idea and cast about for materials" (ibid.).

Day was a native-born Indian all right, but was faced with the same situation as European collectors "Where was an old story-telling woman to be got?" The one he had known and based his fictional character on was long dead, but "after a great deal of search" he found his "Gammer Grethe—Not half so old as the Frau Viehmännin [*sic*] of Cassel—in the person of Bengali woman, who, when a little girl and living in her heathen home, had heard many stories from her old grandmother. She was a good storyteller but her stock was not large" (ibid., viii–ix). He got other tales from "a Brahman, a barber, an old servant." As a collector his choice of narrators was much like a British collector's, but interestingly, he too was collecting stories of people he considered "heathen," just as Anna Liberata narrated stories of Hindu society.

As for his method—he heard the stories and wrote them in English when he returned home. He heard more than he published, because he "rejected a great many." These "appeared to me to contain spurious additions to original stories which I had heard" (ibid., ix). Having thus compiled his collection, Day "inscribed . . . this little book" to Richard Carnac Temple. In turn, Day's collection was much appreciated by Temple and other British collectors, and it stands out in the history of Indian folkloristics because of its unique author and his method. However, he was not so alone at the scale of the Empire.

Samuel Yosia Ntara of Nyasaland authored *Man in Africa*—a work of fiction but written with the purpose of depicting African life and changes therein. Ntara was "a Nyasaland teacher certificated under the recently introduced educational code there" and was "working on the African staff of the Dutch Reformed Church Mission" (Ntara/Huxley 1934, 9). His father had joined the mission, but died early. Ntara grew up under the care of the mission. He wrote the book in his mother tongue, and the manuscript was translated into English. It received an award in the biography section of the International Institute of African Languages and Cultures in London. The published edition was in English, translated from the manuscript by T. Cullen Young and carrying a foreword by Professor Julian Huxley—both of whom patronized and appreciated a work that had not yet appeared in its original version and language.

Huxley felt that in this book "a white man can learn what it means to live (as his own ancestors at one time must have lived) in a small tribal community, with prescribed custom and ritual" (ibid., 7). Young recognized the fact that the book expressed African literary potential, but also found it important for "all British men and women who, in whatever capacity have to live in contact with Africans in Africa" (ibid., 11). He also explained the story for the completely uninitiated reader and wished that Ntara had ended the story in another fashion: "But we have to be content with what we have and the author's [Ntara's] purpose in taking the line he has is clear. He has to show the youth of Nthondo in its darkest colour; neglect, contempt and ingratitude to the parent least deserving of such treatment; the mother" (ibid., 13). This is indeed a complex text in its construction. Was Ntara trying to conform to the image already present, or was he writing under the influence of his adopted faith—these are questions difficult to answer from the materials we have. It is also possible that his images are being misunderstood completely. An analysis of this text awaits the attention of an Africanist-folklorist.

We have earlier, in the section on official method, seen Rattray's awareness of the problems in the theory and practice of prescribed methods. Those realizations were based on his earlier experience of collecting Chinyanja folklore. While working on *Hausa Folk-Lore* Rattray was in the Gold Coast among the Hausa. He wanted to collect folklore here, too, and this time found a novel way to resolve the problems connected with the recording of oral texts. This solution emerged from the resources of the Hausa society. "[Mr. Rattray's] design was to compass two ends at once—to obtain trustworthy linguistic material, and to explore the inner secrets of the Hausa mind—by giving a somewhat novel turn to an old and approved method," says Professor Marrett of Oxford University in his introduction to Rattray's book *Hausa Folk-Lore* (1913, v). Marrett tells us, "Mr. Rattray's happy thought, then, was to remedy the practical shortcomings of the standard method by finding some one who, as it were, could dictate to himself; who, in other words, could successfully combine the characters of story-teller and reporter in his single person" (ibid., vi). This happy thought had emerged from the presence of an educated class of people literate in Arabic among the Hausas. Marrett learned from Rattray that "A malam of the best class possesses all the literary skill which a knowledge of Arabic and Arabic script involves. None the less, he remains thoroughly in touch with his own people, a Hausa of the Hausas. In his hands, therefore, the traditional lore loses nothing of its authentic form and flavour. In short, the chance of literary manipulation may be ruled out."

Rattray thus employed "For the present work the services of a learned MĀLAM, by name MĀLAM *Shaihu*" (xii). This MĀLAM produced the work on which Rattray's *Hausa Folk-Lore* (1913) is a translation. Rattray tells us that "He [Shaihu] himself wrote down, or translated from manuscripts in Arabic, such information as was required. Much of the work contained in the present volumes involved, first a translation from Arabic into Hausa, secondly, a transliteration of the Hausa writing, and thirdly, a translation into English from the Hausa" (ibid., xii). The manuscript was a masterpiece of calligraphy.

It was a work of art, but Marett emphasized its functional value, "For, apart from its value as a masterpiece of artistic penmanship, this clear and, I understand, correct calligraphy must prove of great assistance to European students of Hausa to whose official lot it falls to wrestle with the productions of native scribe" (ibid., vii). Rattray was much appreciated because his method "manages to dispense with the middle man of another mental type, and brings us in direct contact with the native intelligence as it witnesses to itself" (Marrett for Rattray 1913, vii–viii).

Rattray explains in an "author's note" his use of Malam:

There will thus be no room for embellishments or errors creeping in, as is liable to be the case when the investigator has had to rely on the vagaries of his cook, "boy," or other interpreter for his information. It follows that such a collection will be of more value from the anthropological standpoint. Indeed, of late years many collections of native folk-lore compiled according to this method have been called into being by the demand created by this new science of anthropology. . . .

Stories and traditions collected through the medium of an interpreter are amusing, and might prove of interest in the nursery (though much would have to be omitted or toned down, as savage folk-lore is often coarse and vulgar according to our notions, and hardly fit pour les jeunes filles); but for the student of anthropology such collections cannot be considered to possess much value. (Rattray 1913, x–xi)

The novelty of Rattray's method might have transcended some colonial boundaries had he asked Malam Shahiu to write on the stories, on his experience and method of writing the tales of his oral tradition. There is no text of this nature, and if we look at Rattray's novel method in this light we see yet another instance in which an educated associate and the actual compiler of texts is reduced to the position of a clerk. This was not the only instance in which a native associate did major works. For his last work, *The Tribes of the Asante Hinterland* (1932), his associate was Victor Aboya, who had been educated at various missions and was in 1928 teacher to one of the Fathers (Alleman and Parker 2005, 108). "Not only was he Rattray's host and principal informant in the Zuarungu District, he wrote an extensive treatise on Nankani social life in the vernacular that in his own English translation was incorporated verbatim into *Tribes of the Ashanti Hinterland*. Rattray's earlier writing is characterized by a scrupulous avoidance of any modern, urban influence" (ibid., 108). Apparently, Aboya's text was livelier, but Rattray is quick to assert his authority and says of Aboya, "He has done so faithfully and without any attempt to impress us by airing or dragging in his later acquired European knowledge" (quoted in Allmam and Parker 2005, 109). It is remarkable how colonial officers continuously try to "weed out" European influences from their informants, though it is precisely because of those influences that they are chosen as "associates." The chief of these ways is to manipulate the identity of the native associate or author. The name of the game was *identity*: the *identity* as storyteller, translator, collector, and scholar of folklore was clearly reserved for the British partner in the game.

Rattray's novel method also had parallels. Mrs. Fisher also thought of using the natives as writers:

> *During many years spent in Toro and Bunyoro, I prevailed on the respective kings, Daudi Kasagama and Andereya Duhaga, to undertake to write the history of their country. This was no light task for them, as they had no very clear idea of the subject themselves, and were only just learning to wield the pen. However, they readily took up with the suggestion, and called in from the distant villages, and from the solitude of mountains, some of the old witch-doctors, who perforce had been obliged to forsake their old means of livelihood, or practice it in those regions where the onflowing tide of Christianity had not yet reached....*
>
> *The work was a novel and laborious task to these two dusky potentates, who, day after day, sat in their crude studies, writing as rapidly as they could, while the quaint, withered up, skin-clad ancients squatted on the floor, and related the legends that had been handed down by the generations of sages before them.*
>
> *Writing is quite a newly-acquired art introduced by the missionaries; no traces of calligraphy or inscriptions being found among these peoples ... a history remarkably analogous in form to that of the ancient Egyptians.* (Fisher 1911, v–vi)

Fisher tells us how she organized these materials: "The chapters ... are merely a translation from their own writings; and I have tried as far as possible to translate the text literally. *Heaps of non-essential details have had to be cleared away,* and in many cases modification been made, or passages entirely discarded, to purify the story and render it suitable reading to the general public" (ibid., vi–xiii, emphasis added).

From a common man to the royalty, any native could be the narrator of stories that would define people, nations, and cultures. Indeed, the combinations are interesting for their own sake, British collector and native folk as narrators, or British collectors and native intellectuals, or British collectors and native royalty.

An example of native intellectuals as folktale providers is that of Pandit Natesa Sastri of India, who firstly collaborated with Georgiana Kingscote and later published an independent collection of tales. Sastri was from a generation of Sanskrit teachers employed by the college in Madras to teach Indian languages to British officials. Bearing all marks of the traditional intellectual authority of a Brahman, Sastri found support from his British patrons and even became a member of the Folk-Lore Society (Blackburn 2005, 168). Surprising but true, the Folk-Lore Society which was the hub of colonial debates had almost no members from among the "native" races of the Empire.

The case of the native collectors or producers of works of folklore or folkloristic nature in the colonies accounts for a small number of collections and implies the lack of opportunities available to native collectors at one level, and at another the thrust of the method—whereby translation was the first and final aim. These collections were required not for the colonies, but for the metropolises—the arena of which the colonial rulers were the sole masters. From first to last any native collector required the patronage of a British man or woman to be able to produce these works within the international context of folkloristics. The "independence" of these works can also be questioned at the level of theory and method. Their perspectives are often evidences of the hegemony of colonial education and ideology. Day seemed to be proving that his knowledge of European folkloristics was his best qualification for being taken seriously. Ironically, Temple had suggested the collection of stories told by "old women" to Day because he was a "native." Women as storytellers were most difficult for British men to access across the Empire. Temple was conscious of this, as was Crooke, who lamented that British women had not taken to collecting from women narrators in India, who were the best narrators. Cranville Browne reported from Africa:

> *The best narrators are generally the old women, though it is often difficult to persuade them to display their powers. Once started on a story, however, they tell it really well, with a wealth of descriptive detail and pantomime. The voices of the various characters are carefully imitated, and a considerable amount of dramatic gesture gives life to a narrative, the crucial point of the story being usually emphasized by a most impressive howl, shriek or jump.*

In fact, for a childish audience it would be difficult to improve on one of these ladies as a story-teller. (Browne 1925, 209)

This is a remarkable feature of colonial folkloristics—although women in the colonized societies were important as narrators, and collectors were aware of this reality, yet they could only record that these narrators could not readily be accessed by them. Obviously, the boundaries of language and culture were higher between "native" women narrators and foreign men collectors than between men as collectors and narrators.

In this context, Temple asked Day, a native who knew English well, to collect stories narrated by old women. In all probability he would have thought that Day's nativeness would make access to women narrators possible, as he and Steel expressed in the preface to their 1884 edition of *Wide Awake Stories*: "Bengal Folk-tales are by a native from natives, but the narrators were few" (ibid., ix).[9] Day apparently saw himself in the likeness of a British collector, as the images he invoked, including the unavailability of women as narrators (though he found one), were much the same as in the British writings.

Malam Shaihu was Rattray's solution to the problem of differential speed of writing and narrating: someone who could "dictate to himself." The malam was not only dictating his oral text to himself for the purpose of writing down, but was also dictating a new method and purpose of writing to himself. The issue for the British officials essentially was how to collapse the boundaries between native folklore and foreign method. With this aim they sometimes encouraged and supported some "natives" to take on a more active role in the production of folklore texts. In this process it was not just a merger of languages whereby one text transformed into the other, but the confrontation of two knowledge systems in which the conclusion was pre-determined: that the "native" system be conceptualized and systematized in the order of another knowledge system.

Fisher's native royal writers had only *recently* learned to write at all, and they had to use the skill to record the oral narratives of their own people. How can we understand this process of transformation of orality into writing? Do we have the required tools to understand how the fact that the person recording was just beginning to write influences the record? And if one may be allowed more inquisitive thought, then: what would have been the speed of their writing? Certainly, their narrators also observed them performing this new role and skill; how did they respond to it? We have no more clues to this fantastic situation of recording folklore than mentioned. Where shall we place these transformers of orality in the history of folkloristics or of ethnography of literacy?

CONCLUSION

The study of the methods of folklore collection practiced within the British colonial Empire presents a very vibrant phase of folklore collection. This vibrancy has been defined until now by the volumes of materials collected, but this vibrancy should be defined by its plurality. There is no one method, but methods. There are different types of collectors, different kinds of narrators, working in different linguistic contexts with a variety of resources, and in lack of them. There are instances of recording being a very simple process involving only two people and there are instances of it being an elaborate process spread over vast geographical areas and involving the use of colonial bureaucracy. Already in the late nineteenth century there are clear differentiations between scholarly and nonscholarly collections, but in retrospect we can see a lot of overlap.

The only constant feature of colonial methodology is the search for a method to document the folklore of foreign tongues. By the late nineteenth century a consensus regarding the scientific method had emerged whereby word for word documentation, transcription, transliteration, and translation were expected. Every collector, including the amateurs, guaranteed this process, some proved it by providing transcriptions/transliterations (Temple, Doke). The details of the process, the admitted "pruning away" of "redundancies," and the problems mentioned make it doubtful whether the text was as it existed in the oral tradition or whether or how it had been changed in this special situation by any one or all involved in the process.

Criticism of their method existed in their own time as well, as R. E. Dennett noted in 1910: "Administrators and missionaries are often blamed for adopting methods of administration or evangelising which we all know are not suited to the uplifting of the Negro race. Destructive criticism of such methods is easy, and in this case, where both parties have sincerely done their best, quite unnecessary" (ibid., vii). The same could have been said of their folklore collection methods, that they were not suited to the folklores of the colonized nations because they were not intended for them. The criticism on the scientific value of this material is not unrelated to the stage at which the discipline of folklore was. In 1912 Crooke pointed to this stage in his presidential address to the annual meeting of the Folk-Lore Society, London: "Since the Foundation of our Society we have steadily advanced our frontiers" (ibid., 15). He referred to the definition of folklore by William John Thoms, given in 1846 as the study of "antiquities and archaeology" as a happy inspiration, but added that "in the stage which we have now reached this definition is inadequate, and in popular estimation gives an imperfect idea of the work on which we are engaged. In the first place, *it limited our enquiries to the people of these islands*; secondly, it connotes the stage of collecting isolated facts to undertake at the outset of our career, not the arrangement and co-ordination of recorded material to which our efforts are now specially directed" (Crooke 1912, 15–16, emphasis added). Indeed, the exposure and engagement with folklores of different cultures had contributed to the growth of the concept, and it had moved far away from the collection of "popular antiquities" as it had been perceived on the British Isles. Crooke had himself made the journey between 1878 and 1896 in India—from the collection of "agricultural terminology" to a collection of folktales far ahead of its time in system and organization. As in his own journey, there were many steps involved that remained outside the discourse in his time, and even later on. One of the most important aspects of the colonial methodology is the interaction it generated between the colonial rulers and the colonized subjects. Indeed, some important lessons had been learned by the experience of many people put together.

Clearly, Thoms's definition and the folklore science prior to folklore collection in and from the colonies were more suited to "local histories" of European rural populace, as Walter Mignolo would say, and in the process of collecting and publishing folklores of the colonized subjects from around the world the definition of folklore and folklore's research methods expanded and became "global designs," again in the sense Walter Mignolo uses the term. Following Mignolo, I argue that the above thesis is not about globalization of European ideas or about Eurocentrism. Folklore science expanded because of the challenges provided by the varied colonial contexts, by engagement with varied contexts, and by the involvement of many people from colonized societies. European folkloristics was not capable of dealing with the oralities in different continents, or, it was not an international science as we know it today. It became international outside of the European continent, and came back to Europe as a more matured, though far from flawless, science.

After nearly six decades of colonial folklore scholarship, Charlotte Burne could advise folklorists through her *Handbook of Folk-Lore*, published in 1914: "whatever be the scene of operations, the first requisite in collecting folklore is to enter into friendly relations with the folk. Anything in the way of condescension, patronage, or implied superiority will be a fatal barrier to success, and any display of wealth in dress or equipage should be avoided" (6). She further emphasizes "simple, genial manner," "compliance with the local rules of etiquette and courtesy are needful" as necessary for success. She talks of cultural relativism and the need "to discover the underlying idea, as Miss Kingsley puts it" (7). Ironically, Burne's handbook, though based on the experiences of many collectors from the colonies, and constantly referring to their works, gives no idea of the arrogance colonial collectors practiced in the field and reflected in their writings. At best, it seems like a good liberal advice to the contrary. Burne remains silent on the privileges of power that came almost invariably to the collectors in the colonies and became integral parts of their method.

The colonial folkloristic discourse has been perceived as a monolithic discourse whereby the British collectors were the sole forces behind these collections. What we find is a lively engagement by various people for a variety of reasons. It also includes the emergence of native collectors of folklore across the Empire. While the British folklorists did link up with each other scientifically, personally, and as colleagues in the Folk-Lore Society, their native associates were probably not even aware of each other's identities. Postcolonial folkloristics, too, has not seen them as a "group." They are a "group" without a common national, linguistic, or cultural identity. I would argue that they should be seen as a group to understand the international nature of colonial folkloristics not only from the point of view of the British collectors, but also from that of the native associates. Unfortunately, we have only a few articulations of the associates about the British collectors, or their own motivations, strategies, or contributions. We can only place the bits of information available on some of them to see what their position was in a system of which they were also part—the Empire.

Ram Gharib Chaube is the only such associate whose personal capacities made him leave behind a record that can become his identity. Crooke's relationship with Chaube has yet to find a parallel in the colonial folklore scholarship, such that it lets Chaube be acknowledged as co-author of this unpublished collection, but after more than a century (Naithani 2002a and 2006a). He was neither an anthropological object reproducing texts out of memory, nor someone who had been trained by Crooke. Chaube was part of the execution of a scientific method where his and Crooke's different capabilities combined to produce a richer collection than could have been possible for either of them independent of the other. What differentiates him from Chaina Mull or Malam Shaihu or Daudi Kasagama and Andereya Duhaga is his exceptional ability in many languages, including English, and his genius that he could see the role he was playing with a sense of historical distance and subvert it with intellectual means. The realization could only drive him to insanity. The colonial power structures of knowledge were too intricate to be handled by an individual like Chaube, or even Crooke. That network was spread across many continents, but was finally controlled by publishing houses, general readers, and academic institutions in the metropolis of the Empire. In this network there was place made for Ntara and for Day, because their independence was the best proof of their subservience, or rather, the evidence of the hegemony of western knowledge systems. Even Sastri was acceptable because he fulfilled the Orientalist image of a Brahman Sanskrit scholar. But there was no place for Chaube—who was neither a clerk, nor a Christian convert, but an independent scholar by choice, prolific in work and rationalist in thought. He too was exposed to European folkloristics, but he engaged with it in the scientific spirit of debate and discussion. His only credit could have been of co-author, but Crooke did not publish the collection. And he did not recognize Chaube in other publications. It remains unknown whether he even heard of Chaube's insanity and death in 1914. Chaube's fate was not essentially different from other colonial associates whose contributions to colonial folkloristics remain unidentifiable, but he represents certain extremes of colonial scholarship which may not have been experienced by all. He is the exception that proves the rule.

"Methods" constitute the most diverse aspect of colonial folkloristics. The entanglement of folkloristic method with objective and subjective sociopolitical positions is clearly evident. However, the "problems" of fieldwork, transcription, and translation faced by the colonial collectors and the myriad ways they devised to overcome the problems of textualizing orality reflect the immense growth that folkloristics as a field of study experienced under colonialism.

CHAPTER 4

Theory

Colonial Theories of Folklore

> For above all things a collector of folklore should work independently of theory.
> BURNE 1914, 5

> ... there is no practice without theory, however much that theory is suppressed, unformulated or perceived as "obvious."
> BELSEY 1980, 4

The British colonial collectors are famous for having declared their inability (for lack of time) to theorize upon the folklore materials collected by them. Indeed, there is no formulated theory—neither by the colonial folklore collectors, nor by later scholars. Richard Dorson has detailed the chronology of publications and perceptions separately for India and Africa (Dorson 1968), but has not attempted a theoretical abstraction on colonial folkloristics. In contrast to these claims, close reading of colonial texts lets me propose that colonial collectors constantly offered theoretical abstractions of folklore.

"Theory" in folkloristics is that particular frame in which any collector defines the relationship between "folk" and their "lore." Consequently, this definition plays the role of leitmotiv in the interpretation of texts, performance, and the context. Without the articulation of the relationship between folk and lore, there would be no discipline of folkloristics, only textualized orality. Herein lies the importance of J. G. Herder and the Brothers Grimm. Herder established the connection between language, nation, and spirit (1846), and the Grimms established the connection between folklore and the cultural identity of a nation. In the context of these formulations, their works gained socio-political significance. To understand the theory of colonial folkloristics,

I propose to use the Grimms' introduction to *Children's and Household Tales* (*Kinder—und Hausmärchen,* hereinafter KHM) as the point of comparison. The Grimms' text is not only chronologically older, but also considered the inspiration behind international folkloristics, including colonial folkloristics. I do not wish to challenge this claim to the inspiring nature of the Grimms' text, but want to show how colonial folkloristics was outside the scope of romantic theory. It grew outside of the romantic theory and this difference will be visible, if we keep in mind the basic tenets of the romantic folklore theory as stated in the writings of the Grimms.

The introduction to KHM defines folklore in categories of pastoral life and nature imagery: as the crops that survive after the storm, as the cultural inheritance of a people, and as shared cultural inheritance, the sign of cultural unity and national identity of the people. The people themselves are pastoral, their lore is not born of artificial art, but of natural poetic capacities of human beings, the folk and their lore are pure and simple.

In the following I will abstract theoretical principles from colonial writings on folklore and substantiate them with relevant examples, excerpts, and exceptions. Before that, however, let us understand what the position of theory and theorists was in the colonial world. First of all, we must remember the scale of colonial folklore scholarship: British collectors and their "native" associates compiling collections from the "field" in Asia and Africa, British collectors publishing them in England and then the world of English-language general readers, scholars, and learned bodies spread all across the world. And second, we need to keep in view the historical time in which these works emerged: from the middle of the nineteenth century to the middle of the twentieth century. Its peak period was the last two decades of the nineteenth and the first three decades of the twentieth centuries. In the first quarter of the twentieth century it was interrupted by World War I, and in the second by World War II and the rising freedom struggles in the colonies. We can see the influence of the changing times in the theoretical perceptions. The theory of colonial folkloristics exists in fragments, which are parts of an unarticulated larger whole. These fragments can be interlinked to articulate the theory of colonial folkloristics post-phenomenon.

I would like to point out, and as an important fact, that the colonial folklore collectors and writers who were officials and missionaries in the colonies never gained the status of "theoreticians" back at home, although it was they who "knew" the fields. Contrary to the way the positions of these collectors have been seen with reference to the theoreticians in England, I am going to proceed from the "theoretical" concerns and formulations of the collectors themselves and the way they established a certain relation with the overarching theories of the theorists at home. I wish to present not a view of different folklores from the meeting halls of the Folk-Lore Society, but a view of the meeting halls of the FLS from different colonies. This latter view from the colonies may not be the "native" view, but that of the colonial official; yet it is a view from the colony. It is important to take note of the fact that colonial collectors were long-time residents of the colonies, not visitors, as Roscoe was "a scholar who had the advantages of more than a decade's residence in the country, language fluency, and invaluable 'contacts' with sympathetic, and powerful local authorities" (Rowe 1967, 166), and it can be assumed that their opinions were also influenced by their immediate surroundings.

This view from the colonies also does not presuppose any contradiction or rivalry between the collectors and theorists; in fact, much collaboration can be cited. "The Frazer collection at Trinity College Library, Cambridge, contains over 140 letters which Frazer wrote to the missionary anthropologist John Roscoe. Roscoe was with the CMS in Buganda from 1881 to 1909, and it was Frazer who first interested him in ethnographic work and guided his research" (Ray 1984, 397). Commenting on Roscoe's association with Frazer, Rowe says that Roscoe thanks "Professor James Frazer at Cambridge for help and guidance 'during eighteen years' and for proof-reading *The Baganda*. It is not difficult to see Frazer's concern for the accurate recording of a vast array of 'culture traits' reflected in Roscoe's works.... Though Frazer's ideas undoubtedly affected Roscoe's outlook, they did not determine his findings. Contrary to Frazer's expectations, Roscoe did not conclude that Buganda was ruled by a system of 'divine kinship'" (Rowe 1967, 164).

My attempt is to leave the overarching theories of anthropology and philology and see the fragments of theory that emerge from and during the act of collection—an attempt to approach the subject from the side of praxis.[1] In the previous chapter we saw that most of the collectors found the given theoretical premises too limited to deal with the actual process of collection. Therefore, we shall proceed from the analysis of the writings by the colonial collectors. The debates in the Folk-Lore Society have been summarized by Dorson (1968). His analysis refers to the major philological and anthropological theories that dominated the meetings of the Society. These meetings were held in London, where folklore collectors from the colonies came across each other and with the folklorists and anthropologists based in the academic institutions in the United Kingdom. The writings of the colonial collectors comprise their empirical observations, classification of materials collected, conclusions drawn regarding the mind of the "natives" on the basis of their folklore, and engagement with overarching theories formulated by "armchair" theorists back at home. In order to articulate the theory of colonial folkloristics, three aspects of colonial folklore scholarship need to be studied: empirical theory, classification and declassification of texts, and interpretative theories.

EMPIRICAL THEORY

Empiricism plays a philosophical and a functional role in colonial folkloristics. Indeed, it was never so important for collectors like Herder or the Grimms to describe their narrators and narrative situations in vivid details. The international situation of the colonial collectors motivated them to describe the place and the narrators behind their collection. In the absence of the photographic medium as an easily available tool for recording empirical realities, the description had a crucial role to play: to attract the readers to the text. An important part of colonial folklore theory was sketching out the cultural life of the colonized subject for the knowledge and information of the middle-class readers back at home. Folklore collectors sketch out "another" Empire for us by their description of the narrative situations. The importance of this unit lies in the fact that it becomes the basis of analyses for the collector, and for us a record of different narrative situations. In the narrative situation I would also include the author's description of himself and his situation in the colony, because this too is an element in the reception of the narratives and interpretations thereof. Once again, it is not my intention to cite every description, but those that reflect the variety of narrative situations in the British Empire. Here I would also place the authors as per their main profession, in order to contextualize their interpretations.

"Kashmir as a field of Folk-lore literature is, perhaps not surpassed in fertility by any other country in the world" (Knowles 1888, v). This is how Knowles introduces the region of India where he collected folktales. From the neighboring region of Punjab and around the same time as Knowles, Rev. Swynnerton gives a more detailed picture:

> *They are essentially the tales of the people. They are truly representative of the quaint legends and stories which form the delight of the village hûjra or guest-house on winter-nights, when icy winds are blowing over mountain and plain; when the young men of the village community gather round the blazing logs to be charmed by the voice of some wandering minstrel, to listen*

agape to his incredible descriptions of the miseries and joys of hapless love, or to fantastic tales of giants and fairies; or when the weary wayfarer, if not too spent to sit up, alternates the recital of fictitious wonders by news from the outer world, or commands the attention of auditors as simple as himself, by circumstantial accounts of disastrous chances of his own by flood and fell. (Swynnerton 1892, xi)

Swynnerton's image contains elements of the universal and the particular, but Swynnerton is describing one of the regular narrative situations—the village guest-house, and the minstrels he was referring to were the mirasis, mentioned earlier, and from whom Temple also collected the legends. Swynnerton gets more specific as to the locale and the exact situation of his receiving the tales. "It was at the little village of Ghâzi, on the river Indus, thirty miles above Attock, and upwards of a thousand miles due north of Bombay, that many of these tales were written down from the mouths of the simple narrators themselves" (ibid., xi–xii). Swynnerton has given almost the entire route to the village. In spite of such details he misses crucial information: who wrote the tales from the mouth of the narrator? He does not however stop the description here, but reveals some more of his situation:

There, at the solitary house of my old friend, Thomas Lambert Barlow, Esq., a master of every variety of local dialect, within sight and hearing of the majestic river of history and romance, quite close to the ancient ferry over which Alexander the Great threw his bridge of boats, in a district exclusively pastoral which comprises within its area the fabled mountain of Gandghar, the stronghold of the last of the giants, in the midst of many a ruined temple and fallen fortress pertaining to a nobler race and a former faith, we used to sit late into the night, round the leaping log fire in winter, under the dewless sky in summer, and enjoy hearing, as much as the villagers enjoyed telling, the tales which had charmed their forefathers for scores of generations. (Swynnerton 1892, xii)

The scene of the village guest-house, described earlier by Swynnerton, seems to have been recreated in the bungalow of his civil servant friend. It is obvious that the narrators had been called to this residence. In a paragraph, Swynnerton establishes the link with Alexander's visit to India and describes the scenic beauty of the locale. The collector's locale is itself out of the fairy tales. There is no trace of hardships—personal or otherwise—and the writer seems to be wallowing in the realization of current British control over a land that has been ruled by such great figures as Alexander, Ashoka, and the Mughal emperors.

Swynnerton's portrayal also has elements that constitute the descriptions of the folklore collectors from India. They describe beautiful landscapes from the north (as in Knowles), or the northwest (as in Swynnerton), or from the south (as in Frere and Kingscote), or the central parts of the subcontinent (Gordon). The common narrators and professional wandering narrators are available, are invited at the residence or the camp, and they narrate in a scenic, relaxed atmosphere, much enjoyed by the collector himself.

The collectors from India also describe their narrators: Frere's animated Anna, Stokes's pantomiming ayahs, Dracott's servants with attitudes, Temple's professional narrators who needed a dose of opium before beginning, Swynnerton's unnamed "villagers," Crooke's cooks, peons, clerks, and the professional narrator Akbar Shah Manjhi ("a quaint old blind man" who came to Crooke's residence and the camps, stayed around for many days, and narrated in the evenings to Crooke and Chaube). Crooke's butler had orders to keep the narrator well fed.

The collectors from Africa also portray a world that seems to come straight from the stories:

> *Here ghosts from long-dead worlds have made their home*
> *Dark Mangrove boughs form window frame and door.*
> *Of whispering wind-swayed leaves is built each wall:*
> *And the breathless silence is peopled all*
> *With echoes and dreams.*
> ....
> *Through breeze and storm-wind, myriad voices call—*
> *Mid glints and gleams, fierce sun's or moon's soft beams—*
> *Seeking, in our deaf ears, to breathe the Lore,*
> *Gleaned, in the days ere Greece and Rome were born,*
> *From long-forgotten worlds and Faiths outworn. (Talbot 1923, v)*

For Talbot, the reasons lie within the locale—in its geography and the mysterious atmosphere and in the antiquity of this lore—it is older than that of Greece and Rome. This mysterious atmosphere is in the gaze of the folklore collector: he sees this world as a surreal place where ghosts from bygone eras roam around freely, probably implying the widespread ancestor-worship. In other words, the writer is expressing the theory of survivals in verse and metaphorical language. And as its mark of distinction the collector points out that the lore of the British colony is older than that of Greece and Rome. The collector goes a step further and says that here in the colony the living, in their conservative lifestyle, are shadows of the dead. By inversion, the colony adds a historical depth and resultant distinction to the British *Empire*, while the particular colony is simultaneously presented many centuries backward as compared to Britain, because it still lives like it did. E. Sherman Oakley makes a similar comparison in the context of India:

> *The glory that was Greece and the grandeur that was Rome have passed away, and their sites only are left as relics of the past. India, on the contrary, has the more vivid charm of a treasure yet unexplored, a storehouse of existing marvels, a vast and complex field for research of every kind. Many secrets of bygone eras are yet to be wrung from its buried monuments and unpublished manuscripts. Here the ancient world yet lives on in the daily lives of men. Customs, cults, and ideas that have perished from the memory of the rest of the human race are here in full force. India is the land that above all has power to stir imagination. (Oakley 1905, 9)*

The similarity in the depiction of the two locales is striking: both are older, and therefore more distinguished than Greek and Roman civilizations, and in both places (India and Africa) ancient worlds or ghosts live into the present times.

The stories may have been old, but they were being told in the collectors' time. The descriptions of storytelling are vivid in the collections of African folklore.

> *Perhaps it may interest you to know how a story is told.*
>
> *Imagine, then, a village in a grove of graceful palm trees. The full moon is shining brightly upon a small crowd of Negroes seated round a fire in an open space in the centre of the village. One of them has just told a story, and his delighted audience demands another. Thus he begins:*
>
> "*Let us tell another story: let us be off!*"
>
> *All then shout:* "*Pull away!*"
>
> "*Let us be off!*" *he repeats.*
>
> *And they answer again:* "*Pull away!*" *Then the story teller commences.* (Dennett 1967, 25)

Dennett quotes this interesting style of beginning the narration among the Fjort, but he does not tell us where and how he witnessed it.

The atmosphere of storytelling is building, and J. Torrend takes us into another session:

> THE TYPICAL BANTU TALE: *It consists of two distinct parts, one narrated, mostly in the form of dialogues, the other sung.... Of the two parts the more important is the one that is sung, so much so that in many tales the narrative is to it no more than a frame is to a picture.*
>
> *The part which is sung is not only free to borrow words from any language known to the singer, but is supposed, moreover, to understand and interpret the language of birds, other animals, and nature in general. It is composed of a monologue, or a dialogue, and a chorus....*
>
> *These little melodramas are, in fact, such a power in Central Africa.... An evening with the phonograph repeating some of the very tales printed in this book has even been found to be far more interesting for throngs of natives than grand exhibitions of magic lantern. (Torrend 1921, 3–5)*
>
> THE AIM OF OUR STORY-MAKERS—*As a rule, the Mukuni tale is tragic. The more versatile Tonga are able to compose comic stories as well. What Mukuni and Tonga story-tellers have in common . . . is their intention, not only to make their young hearers happy, but also, and above all, "to instruct." Every tale, from their point of view, is a lesson, it may be of a principle of law, or of civilized manners as they understand them, or even of religious dogma.... (ibid., 5–6)*
>
> ORIGIN OF THESE TALES—*For all we know, some of these tales, both Tonga and Mukuni, may be as old as the hills; of others it cannot be proved that they are not as recent as the invasion of Africa by railways and flying machines. What is certain is that most of them are losing their hold on the natives with the advance of European civilization, which concentrates their thoughts on money at the expense of the old happy-go-lucky ideals. (Torrend 1921, 6)*

Torrend mentions use of the phonograph for recording oral performance, though any clue to the whereabouts of this record is not given. He inadvertently makes a comparison with the magic lantern—the precursor to cinema. His reference brings to the fore the emergence of a conflict between media of storytelling. Orality was not only confronted with print or written word, but also audio-visual media. Collectors were already expressing the need to record on phonograph and cinematograph, and films would soon be competing for space with oral storytelling. Rev. Smith also portrayed his Ila-speaking narrator vividly: "It is at evening around the fires that the tales are told, especially on dark nights, when the people cannot dance so comfortably. Many of the tales are known far and wide, others in lesser areas. But, however often the people hear them, they never seem weary of repetition. They never say, 'Oh, that's an old tale,'... with no trace of boredom come in with their ejaculations just at the right points, take, it may be, a sentence out of the narrator's mouth, or even keep up a running echo of his words" (Smith and Dale 1920, 336). These narrators of Africa, like the mirasis of Punjab, or Akbar Shah Manjhi of Awadh, also did not know the way their narratives would be interpreted and become the definition of their culture.

Another very interesting situation of storytelling was described by Mary Kingsley: "It may at first strike the European as strange, when, listening to the trial of a person for some offence before either a set of elders, or a chief, he observes that the discussion of the affair soon leaves the details of the case itself, and busies itself with the consideration of the conduct of a hyena and a bush-cat, or the reason why monkeys live in trees, or some such matter" (Kingsley, in Dennett 1897, xi). She identified the so-called law stories which were "equivalents to leading cases" in the English legal system, and were cited in defense of one's arguments in legal trials. These stories had a formulaic ending: "and the people said it was right" (ibid.). "Naturally, the art in pleading lies in citing the proper story for the case," says Kingsley (ibid.).

The descriptions of the colonial folklore collectors bring out a few things: the native situations of storytelling, the colonial/contemporary situations of storytelling, ways of storytelling, and the collector's personal situation in the process of storytelling. I would like to draw some generalizations from the individual cases as represented. As such they do not apply to all in equal measure.

1. Folk are ignorant of the modern world.
2. Folk and folklore live in remote places which are romantic, but also dangerous, inaccessible, and too hot.
3. Folklore performers are amazingly creative and capable. Their relationship with their audience is live, constant, and part of their performative style.
4. People as audience play their role in the performance.
5. The wealth of folklore is in contrast to the poverty, primitiveness, and backwardness of the people.

6. Folklore has more functions than mere entertainment—both those which were part of other institutions, like law and religion, and those that were part of social gatherings.
7. Folklore performers may be banned by the colonial administration because of their associated practices not acceptable to the colonial state. The same performers may be summoned for the purposes of folklore collection. In other words, the performance and the text can be disconnected from their other roles in society.
8. For a colonial collector, "folk" are all natives—from royalty to the poorest person.

The descriptions of empirical realities cited earlier in the text require a critical glance to notice that the following are generally missing:

- The exact places, dates, or years.
- Names of narrators and their relationship to the collector.
- Details of the audience.
- Names of associates or those recording or those translating/explaining the narrative to the collector.
- Resistance to colonialism or nature of cooperation.

CLASSIFICATION AND DECLASSIFICATION

Classification of oral texts is an important task of folklore theory. Had the Grimms used another word for German folktales instead of Märchen, the history of folkloristics would have been substantially different, and Märchen would not have become its most popular word. Before that it was a word known to the German speaking folk and used by them. Let us see in the following what the colonial collectors did with the Asian, African, and Australian terms classifying different genres of oral expressive cultures.

The colonial collectors of Africa attempted a classification of tales they collected more often than their Indian counterparts. In the classification of tales it is important to note that often classifications were available in the language of the folklore concerned but that the colonial collectors did not mention them. In most cases it cannot even be ascertained whether the majority of these collectors were aware of the terms and categories. Some collectors mentioned the original categories, but most often made their own classifications. In the following I will present those examples which are more detailed than the general ones.

Doke, the collector of the Lamba folktales, was one of those who mentioned the native classification system, but then offered his own:

> *Lamba folklore is classified by the natives in two ways, according to the mode of recitation. First and foremost comes the prose story, called Icisimikisyo. The other, which, for want of a better term, is translated as "Choric Story," is variously called by the natives,—Ulusimi, Icisimi, Akasimi and Akalawi. This is a prose story interspersed with songs. The stories are mostly recited by the women and girls, the verse parts being chanted in a way which is not without its charms, especially to the native audience hanging on every word. Some ten examples of these choric stories are given in this collection. (Doke 1927, XII)*

These forms were integral to the way audiences were expected to participate in the act of narration, and thus the "native" classificatory terms were composite categories. "One noticeable feature of Lamba stories, and indeed of all Bantu folk-lore is the amount of repetition, as instanced in Story LXVIII, but this repetition has the effect of working up the audience to a pitch of excitement, as they watch for the slightest divergence in the narrative to indicate the turning-point of the story" (ibid.). However, for analysis he avoided this classification system and presented another.

> *Lamba stories may be divided roughly into four kinds:*
>
> *(1) Animal Tales, in which the animals converse as human beings. These center around the adventures of Mr. Little Hare. In these Central African Tales one finds the pure fount of the . . .*
> *(2) Tales of village life in which fun is indulged in . . .*
> *(3) Some few stories are proper fairy-tales of lovely princesses and wondrous wealth, which is usually liable to instant disappearance . . .*
> *(4) There is another section of tales dealing with ogres and gnomes, and the weird denizens of the forest. . . . (Doke 1927, XIII–XIV)*

The differences in the two classification systems are very interesting. While the native classification is based on the two major forms of oral narration, Doke's classification is based on the contents of the stories. Doke's introduction of his own system represents a peculiar feature of colonial folkloristics:

that it dissociated the folklores concerned from their associated meanings, and presented them as texts open for universal interpretation.

A similar classification was offered by Smith and Dale with regard to the tales of the Ila-speaking peoples of Northern Rhodesia: "We have divided the tales into four parts. The first contains etiological or explanatory myths" (1920, 337). The second section was devoted to the tales of Sulwe—the "popular" hare-hero of African narratives. The third and the fourth sections contained "respectively tales of people and animals, and tales of people—mostly fools. These will speak for themselves and do not require much by way of introduction" (ibid., 343). This was more an arrangement of tales into a book, instead of a scientific classification. They casually mention that many of them (tales about people) have

> *a special name given to them, i.e. Kashimi. All the other tales were made, and are told, for amusement, with no didactic purpose, but these have a definite aim. They end with the words: Inzho bamushima, which means, "And so they make a byword of him, put him on record as an example not to be followed." A nagging woman, an ungrateful, cruel son, a querulous wife, a man who hurts himself, a naughty child, silly women who entrust their children to old hags, fools who do not understand—all are put on record as solemn or humorous warnings to the younger generation. (ibid., 343)*

Mary Kingsley suggested a classification for the stories of the Fjort collected by Dennett: "The stories can be roughly divided into three classes (only roughly, because one story will sometimes have material in it belonging to two classes)—legal, historical, and play. You have in this small collection examples of all these. The Nzambi stories are historico-legal; the 'crocodile and the Hen' is legal; 'the Wonderful child' is play-story, and so on" (Kingsley, in Dennett 1897, ix).

Mary Kingsley's category "legal story" was based on her own observation in West Africa, but her other categories also reflect the needs of the Empire which might be fulfilled by the collection of folklore. The principles of social regulations, history of the people concerned, and what occupied the leisure hours of the natives were the areas the knowledge that could be crucial to administration. Kingsley, like many others, considered the majority of the stories to have regulatory authority, while she found that "As a general rule, historical stories are rare among West African tribes; you find more of them among the Fjort . . ." (ibid., ix–x). None of the categories are actually folkloristic. What is evident in these examples is that folkloristic concerns and categories are closely interlinked with the aims of the folklore collection. The classification of tales, or the lack of it, is one historical limitation of the scientific aspects of colonial folkloristics.²

In India, the writings tended more toward an engagement with the overall theoretical approaches and their relation with the stories collected. The overall genres of the collections were clearly defined. Frere's, Stokes's, Steel's, Knowles's, Day's, and Kingscote's collections were made from common or nonprofessional narrators. Some of Swynnerton's stories came from the professional bards, but he rendered them in ordinary prose. Temple collected the stylized narratives from the bards of Punjab, whose act was stylized in terms of text, music, and performance. He called the performed narratives "versified legends" and did not even mention the local categories. Therefore, perhaps, the discussion tended to be more on the relation of these to the European narratives. Yet, Temple's contribution to the study of the versified legend in Punjab will continue to remain meaningful. Moreover, Temple also preserved the manuscripts of translations from the vernacular into Persian by his munshi, Chaina Mull. These may offer unprecedented insights to a scholar with knowledge of Persian. If Temple collected stylized oral narratives, then Crooke made a mammoth collection of the everyday common tale of the vast rural society, and also of the professional narrator of the villages. It is indeed surprising that such vast amounts of folklore in India were collected, were important to the debates and discussion in England, and yet, hardly any classification was attempted. Interest in Indian folktale was largely diverted by the question of whether it was or whether it was not the original version of some European narrative. After his long and winding discussion on Theodor Benfey's theory that India was the original homeland of European folk narratives, Swynnerton tells of his scheme: "I have intentionally thrown my examples together almost haphazard, for my object is to amuse rather than to instruct" (Swynnerton 1892, xv). Even more than the micro-level debate, the overall theme—whether India is or is not the home of all narratives—exhausted the energies required for a full-scale mapping of the types, genres, and functions of the folktale in India. It is as if all the collectors put together were scratching just the surface, some a little more than others. But the contribution of the colonial collectors toward a scientific study of Indian folklore is negligible. In fact, when we consider this aspect we realize that this is a logical result of the colonial methodology—that the collectors collected what they "chanced upon" in the course of their other duties, obligations, and ambitions. The choice was not made on scientific grounds and the effort required for a scientific study of the materials collected was most often not feasible. It is not humility when collectors say that they were not trained collectors, but a fact that has affected the kind of collections we have. The folklore of the entire colonial world was actually categorized in the four macro categories already known to European scholarship: proverbs, stories, riddles and songs, and among these almost all collectors were concerned with stories. The reason was best expressed by Mary Kingsley in her introduction to Dennett's work on folklore of the Fjort, but applies probably to all colonial folklore collectors in other places too: ". . . no one has dealt with the songs, and indeed it would be exceedingly difficult to do so, as in the songs, more than in other native things, as far as I can judge, do you find yourself facing the strange under-meaning in the very words themselves. But, interesting as the songs and riddles are, the proverbs and stories are infinitely the more important portions of the native literature, for in them we get the native speaking to his fellow-native . . ." (Dennett 1897, ix).

INTERPRETATIONS FROM FOLKLORES

> The literature or the lore of any people is a sure indicator of their mental and moral outlook. This is especially true of a people who have no written literature but whose lore has been handed down from generation to generation by word of mouth.
> DOKE 1927, XI

This statement by Doke forms a kind of spinal cord for the body of knowledge created by colonial British folklore collectors. The lore of the people was not only their oral expressive culture, but was more important as a record of the moral and structural fabric of the society concerned. The contours of this body could be exhibited through interpretation of the collected and translated texts. The quintessence of interpretation was the effort to understand the present and the past of the colonized peoples. The interpretations were important because the interest of the reading public was also centered on comprehending what the different peoples of the Empire were like. The interpretations had full chance of becoming popular among and through the successive generations of travelers who would look into these accounts to prepare themselves for their own landing amid some of these peoples.

In contrast to the classifications of tales, the colonial writings on folklore are rich in interpretation of the materials collected throughout the Empire. Almost every collector articulated his or her interpretations of the tales and simultaneously did not articulate the interpretations of the tellers from whom he or she heard the tales. If they did include the tellers' interpretations in their text, then they did so without identifying it as such and transformed it to match with their own ideas. The interpretations of folklore texts has two *leitmotives*: (1) texts as reflective of social-psychological realities, and (2) folklore as record of history.

The first kind of interpretation, texts as reflective of social-psychological realities, is common in the writings of the colonial collectors. They tried to explain the tales by what they had "seen" in the colony of their residence, and vice versa. An excellent example of this is provided by Smith and Dale, the collectors of folklore in *The Ila Speaking People of Northern Rhodesia* (1920). Although materials were collected from all over Africa by many collectors, yet it was the animal tales that attracted the maximum attention and interpretation, and out of these the adventures of Sulwe (the Hare) and Fulwe (the Tortoise). Smith and Dale chose this set of tales for a detailed interpretation. The popularity of this narrative among the British collectors may also be due to the narrative's difference to the famous Indo-European tale of the race between the fast-running rabbit and the slow but steady tortoise. The African narratives also ended in the tortoise winning the race, but the progression of the narrative to that end was very different: "In the famous race between the two animals Fulwe [the tortoise] wins, not by patient running, but by cunningly hiding her family in numbers along the coast, so that whenever Sulwe [the hare] halts to jeer at his rivals he hears a Tortoise ahead of him crying to him to Come on! until after days of running he gives in exhausted, and the Tortoise, as fresh as ever, brings him water from the river that was their goal. And in the last act of this wonderful drama, it is Fulwe who finally beats Sulwe . . ." (Smith and Dale 1920, 340).

The analyses of this tale by the colonial collectors offer an insight into the theoretical paradigms of the colonial folklore scholarship. Establishing the connection between the tales, tellers, and listeners required authentication. In the case of this story the best authentication was its popularity. Smith and Dale collected this story from the Ba-ila and claimed to have witnessed its performances. ". . . He [Sulwe, the Hare] is the most popular of all the dramatis personae. In the minds of the Ba-ila he embodies all subtlety. He is skilful in practical jokes; he is cruel, he is cunning, he is false; a Macchiavel, a Tartuffe, a downright rogue. He should be a despicable character, but the Ba-ila shake and roll about with laughter as they listen, for the hundredth time, to his adventures. Nor can we resist joining in the laughter; he is such a droll creature that we forget his treacherous conduct . . ." (ibid., 339–40). The narrative is being seen and experienced by two subjects, African and British.

On the surface they are part of the same event, but the perceptions of the tale and the event in their minds were different. The writers are conscious of it and draw parallels and narrate personal anecdotes in order to make their readers also get into the narrative:

> *These two creatures, Sulwe and Fulwe, who, in the minds of the Ba-ila, are rivals in cunning and far surpass the other animals, are in many respects the very antithesis the one of the other: the Tortoise is the slowest as the Hare is the swiftest. It is not difficult to understand why the Hare should be regarded as he is. He is extremely wary; as poachers and others in England know, it is most difficult to entrap him. He has the power, more than most animals, of lying low and saying nothing. You may step over him and never know he is there. We were once pitching our tent in the bush—standing with a number of men together, when from out, it seemed, beneath our feet there darted a hare. The incident caused immense excitement among our men, and that night, and for many nights afterwards, it was cited as an example of Sulwe's amazing wisdom. He had come, they declared, especially to study the white man and his ways, and having seen all, had gone off to tell the other animals. . . . The wisdom of Fulwe, the Tortoise, is, on the other hand, founded on its power of shutting itself up tightly in its shell and the difficulty of killing it. So we have two types of cunning—the active and the passive; the one which gains by nimbleness, the other by quiescence; the one goes abroad to seek its victims, the other circumvents those who come to it. And in the estimation of the Ba-ila, the slow-moving, passive, undemonstrative kind of cunning is the one that wins in the long run. (ibid., 340–41)*

Smith and Dale apparently went with the general mood momentarily, but there was another narrative unfolding in their mind; and this narrative they would communicate in writing.

> *In sketching these animals, not Sulwe and Fulwe only, but all the animals in these tales, the Ba-ila are sketching themselves. The virtues they esteem, the vices they condemn, the follies they ridicule—all are here in the animals. It is a picture of Ba-ila drawn by Ba-ila, albeit unconsciously, and valuable accordingly. In the hero, Sulwe, we may find some at least of the characteristics that the African most admires. The tales show that he esteems mind above physical strength, brain above brawn. The Elephant and the Lion are types of the latter, the Hare of the former, and Sulwe always wins; if at last he is beaten it is only by superior cunning. (ibid., 341)*

Connecting their own beliefs, that of people in England, and the African stories, Smith and Dale take us on a long detour into psychoanalyzing the Ba-ila. The story collectors further support their interpretation by citing examples of the "real" heroes in the history of the Ba-ila:

> *In real life among the Bantu, it is not so much a Hector as an Odysseus that prevails; even in those cases where, as with Moshesh and Chaka and Sebitwane, the chief is also a great warrior, he does more by subtlety than by the assegai. The greatest figure in Basuto history is not Moshesh but Mohlomi, the mystic and seer. The most powerful persons, because most feared, among the Ba-ila are the munganga and musonzhi, the doctor and diviner, who with much knowledge have also abundance of wit and cunning. Yes, the Ba-ila appreciate mind, but the type that appeals most to them is the Sulwe type or the Fulwe type: to get the better of one's neighbours without being found out—that is wisdom. We wonder in reading these tales that the great beasts should so readily be deceived; could they not see through Sulwe's specious lying and clumsy stratagems? Our wonder ceases when here, too, we recognize a picture of the people. Along certain lines the Ba-ila are the most credulous of men; the greatest liar finds the readiest credence. We have only to think of the various "prophets" that arise with marvelous claims, and the way in which they jockey the people into parting with their goods, to realize that Sulwe is no overdrawn picture. . . . wonder ceases when . . . we recognize a picture of the people. (ibid., 341–42)*

For a postcolonial reader, "wonder" is in the way in which the picture of a people is created through a set of oral narratives. Smith and Dale specify:

> *This assumes, of course, that the makers of these tales regarded these animals as persons capable of volition. We are not prepared to say that sophisticated listeners to these tales to-day all believe that animals act and speak like men, however eagerly they may receive the tales; but most of the natives would, we believe, accept them as veridical. . . . It was not unnatural for the makers of these tales to ascribe human characteristics to the lower animals, for they did not recognize any psychical difference between them and us. . . . (ibid., 338–39)*

Smith and Dale were conscious of differences, and were willing to consider them. Writing in 1920, the authors were conscious of intercultural aspects of interpretation: "If we cannot always appreciate the humor of these tales, we have to remember that ideas of humor vary according to race. Certainly to the Ba-ila they are full of humor; they roll about and laugh themselves almost into hysterics when they hear the tales" (344). However, the collectors probed further and asked themselves, "What are the things that appeal thus to them [Ba-ila]?" (344). The answers were listed by them and reflect a particular brand of cultural relativism. It is accepted that the other is different, but that "difference" itself defines the other:

> *First of all, they [Ba-ila] find exquisite delight in the buffoonery. The rough, practical jokes of Sulwe, with his absurd dressing up, his slashing and chopping, his breaking of teeth, and all the rest of it, are distinctly humorous to them. And it must be said, too, that to them facility in deception is humorous. Sulwe owes his popularity very largely to his unveracity [sic] and his diabolical skill in deceiving those bulkier than himself. And as with ourselves, the element of incongruity in many of these situations appeals to their sense of humour. The incongruity between Hare and Elephant in point of size, makes them laugh when the little one ties up the big. . . . Smart sayings, clever retorts, and cryptic utterances also appeal to their sense of humour. . . . And they delight in play on words and the mistakes people make in misunderstanding words that are similar in pronunciation but different in meaning. General obtuseness of mind is also humorous to them. It is these things which give point to the stories of fools, of which we give a few examples. (ibid., 344–45)*

Dissociating themselves from a similar pleasure in tales as the "natives," the authors excel in the ambiguity of their comments. The characteristics thus identified in the fictional characters are applicable to the tellers and listeners. The collectors establish the narrators of their tales as rather ridiculous but grant them knowledge, at least a mind that queries at another plane:

> *It is usual to regard savages as uneducated people, and, as far as books are concerned, they certainly are, but in the book of Nature they are well read. . . . They ask not so much, How? as Why? Why are things as they are? Some of the questions are serious enough; certain of them exercise the minds of cultured men among ourselves. Why are monkeys so like and yet so different from men? . . . The answers to these questions are embodied in tales. If the explanations are naïve, they bear witness to considerable powers of observation and reflection, of imagination and humour. . . .*
>
> *As for these explanations, it will be seen that none of them is assigned to any natural cause, but all to personal volition. . . . (ibid., 336–37)*

The tone implies objectivity, and yet the subjective nature and personal comments are all but hidden. Surprisingly, the authors—a combination of the missionary and the official—reach a conclusion about the "common" elements of humanity: "It may be said in conclusion that man's common human heartedness is in these tales. Grief and joy are shown to touch the same chords in their breasts as in ours. How simply, yet how touchingly, are the fundamental human emotions described: the love of parents, the grief that accompanies bereavement, the joy in offspring—these, as well as the jealousy, the envy, the malice of our human nature find place here. Separated by deep gulfs as they are from ourselves in many things, yet across the abysses we can clasp hands in a common humanity" (ibid., 345). The analysis by Smith and Dale is more detailed than others, but is representative of certain ways of interpretation. In his article "The Anthropology of Colonialism," Peter Pels throws light on the broader intellectual context of collectors like Smith and Dale: "[The] Anthropological view of colonialism stressed a combination of the three [modernization, exploitation/domination, and negotiation]" (Pels 1997, 163). We can see these three elements running under the surface of Smith and Dale's text as collection, textualization/translation, and interpretation. They were also among the more knowledgeable of colonial collectors. In their interpretation the folk behind the lore are "primitive" and "oral," they need to be textualized/translated and interpreted for the rest of the world. As we have seen in preceding chapters, Smith and Dale were also aware of the limitations of their record, but they were more confident with regard to their interpretations of the narratives. Their conclusions had a note of finality: ". . . whether it springs from good or evil, it is always a person that affects the destiny. This, one may say, is typical of the higher native thought, that explains things not by mere self-acting dynamism but by the activity of the will" (Smith and Dale 1920, 338).

They made their own classification and said that "animal tales" were the most widespread and constituted the majority of oral narratives. This concerned the form of narrative but, along with the content form, was also subject to interpretation concerning the mind of the narrators. "In these later tales there is apparent a certain straitness [*sic*] of fancy. By taking animals and not men as the usual figures of the tales they are following instinctively a safer path. Animals are a more fluid medium than men" (ibid., 343). So the tales themselves are not of any great craft and art of storytelling, but of the simplest possible resolutions toward expression. Smith and Dale's text is important because it reflected the comments made in other works as well.

Doke, collector of Lamba folktales (1927), expresses himself somewhat differently as he connects the images in the story with the daily life of people. Without using the terms, Doke establishes a one-to-one relationship between "folklore" and "folklife":

> *In all these stories one gets glimpses of the people's village life and thought. One sees the dish of "inshima" porridge, and the bowl of relish, without which they couldn't make a meal. In the hut one sees the citupa or store-loft under the roof, where the man hides away from the goblins. One sees the bundles of thatching-grass standing where Kantanga and his companions speared the ogre. One sees the man carefully covering over his pitfall for game and then the old woman going out with her axe to cut firewood. . . .*
>
> *The natives, too, picture the ogres and animals as living in just such villages and huts, as they themselves do. In a country where darkness reigns as soon as the lamp of the sun goes down, the story, told around the fire at night, takes the place of the arm-chair book in the brilliantly-lighted home. (Doke 1927, XIV–XV)*

Doke affirms that the images created in stories are the images of the physical world of the society they come from. At the mental plane, however, he sees a contradiction: ". . . almost every story carries with it its moral implied if not expressed. It may be surprising to some that, on the whole, these morals are of so high a character. . . . On the other hand, cunning, even unscrupulous cunning is highly praised" (ibid.). Doke touches on the aspects already discussed by Smith and Dale in the same manner, but incidentally adds bits of information completely missing in other writings: "In certain of the stories, too, even adultery is made light of, but that part of the story is usually incidental to something more important in the tale. . . . There are, of course, many tales told by natives of a lascivious nature that are regaled for the laugh which their coarseness prompts; but as far as I can make out, these are modern creations of little moment, and are seldom if ever used by the regular story-teller" (Doke 1927, XV). Doke's moralistic perspective toward erotic lore is clear and not surprising. It is interesting how he almost apologizes for the existence of such stories by calling them "modern creations of little moment."

Mary Kingsley identifies the use of animal stories as "legal stories" and concludes from them:

> *Legal stories . . . are the stories which have the greatest practical value, for in them is contained evidence of the moral code of the African. . . . You will find*

them all pointing out the same set of lessons: that it is the duty of a man to honour his elders; to shield and sustain those dependent on him, either by force of hand or by craft; that violence, or oppression, or wrong done can be combated with similar weapons; that nothing can free a man from those liabilities which are natural to him; and finally, that the ideal of law is justice—a cold, hard justice which does not understand the existence of mercy as a thing apart from justice. For example, a man, woman, or child, not knowing what it does, damages the property of another human being. . . . if it can be proved that the act was committed in ignorance that was not a culpable ignorance, the doer cannot be punished by law. . . . underlying principles of law itself are fairly good. (Kingsley, in Dennett 1897, x–xi)

Kingsley draws some interesting parallels—not with Europe's narratives but with its legal system: "The part these stories play in the administration of justice is remarkable. They clearly are the equivalents to leading cases with us, and just as the English would cite A v. B, so would the African cite some such story as 'The Crocodile and the Hen,' or any other stories you find ending with 'and the people said it was right.' Naturally, the art in pleading lies in citing the proper story for the case—one that either puts your client in the light of a misunderstood, suffering innocent, or your adversary in that of a masquerading villain" (ibid., xi). Kingsley's comments point to the fact that oral narratives play more definite roles but might be considered simple stories out of their social context. The oral narratives of the colonized were subject to complete change of identity in their international *avatar* in the English language. At an overall level they would be seen as reflecting the physical and the mental world of their narrators, but their specific value and role in the societies of their existence would be dissociated from them just like the way the African categories of narratives would be obliterated under the system of understanding introduced by the collectors.

In the very first colonial collection—that of Indian folktales, which a young British woman almost accidentally came to compiling—it was clear that the tales were going to be seen in the larger framework of "reflecting the people who narrate them." Frere draws interesting contrasts between her perception of Indian society and that which is reflected in the tales:

Though varied in their imagery, the changes between the different legends are rung upon very few themes, as if purposely confined to what was most familiar to the people. . . . It is remarkable that in the romances of a country where women are supposed by us to be regarded as mere slaves or intriguers, their influence (albeit most frequently put to proof behind the scenes) should be made to appear so great, and, as a rule, exerted wholly for good; and that in a land where despotism has such a firm hold on the hearts of the people, the liberties of the subject should be so boldly asserted as by the old Milkwoman to the Rajah in "Little Surya Bai," or the Malee to the Rajah in "Truth's Triumph"; and few, probably, would have expected to find the Hindoos owning such a romance as "Brave Sevantee Bai"; or to meet with such stories as "The Valiant Chatteemaker," and "The Blind Man, the Deaf Man, and the Donkey" among a nation which, it has been constantly asserted, possesses no humour, no sense of the ridiculous, and cannot understand a joke. (Frere 1868 [1929], xviii)

Frere appreciates her stories by decrying the society they came from and considers the stories contradictions to social realities, not an invitation for a closer look at the social environment. Georgiana Kingscote sees not contradiction between the two but similarities:

In the fables of the East, especially India, there is one peculiarity, namely, that craft and cunning are more generally rewarded than virtue, and stupidity condemned. This is the national characteristic. The tales of Southern India are as varied as any others, either Eastern or European. Magic and supernatural phenomena play a great part, but are usually assisted by the powers of the gods. This is again a national Hindoo characteristic. The Hindoo would shrink from any undertaking that is not under the patronage of the gods; yet here is a very noticeable feature, namely, that the divinities are treated as entirely secondary in power, interwoven only into a man's daily affairs as a sort of backbone or support in time of need, but to be despised and trampled upon at other times with impunity. This is a natural feature in a nation which has a deity to represent every vice and sin, and lends a certain character to the tales of Southern India different to the folklore of other countries. (Kingscote 1890, xi–xii)

For Kingscote the tales reflect the "national Hindoo characteristics," among which are "craft and cunning." In an argumentative sweep she locates the problem in the nature of (Hindu) religion itself. This is surprising, considering that she was compiling her collection in association with a Brahman scholar of Sanskrit. I wonder if he had anything to do with her introduction—if he ever saw it before publication. The missionary Rev. Charles Swynnerton considers the tales he collected to be older than "history itself," but calls his narrators "rude and unlearned." Temple simply touches his stories with historical-geographical theories, as mentioned earlier, but does not analyze the tales in any detail. Crooke's writings reveal a tendency toward the study of variants, but do not contain interpretation of any story. Interestingly, although "revealing the mind of the people" was the major aim of collecting stories, yet the collectors of Indian folklore did not always dwell on that aspect. They hinted that the tales were connected with the sociological and philosophical viewpoints of the tellers of these tales, but did not elaborate on those ideas. In fact, the folktales also added to the "queer" character of India in the eyes of the British. "India" was a puzzle, and its folklore seemed too varied to be comprehended within interpretations. The writers generally left this job to the readers.

The definition of "culture" of the narrators' society was what constituted interpretation. This basic model of interpretation is the same with regard to Indian and African folklore. In the discussion on Indian folklore, the interpretations tended to be very general. The obvious "similarities" between the Indian and the European narratives also made the tales less "strange." It is not the scientific similarity that is being referred to here, but the structure of narratives, the concept of protagonists, and the events. As Ralston succinctly puts it:

> *Some of the stories in this volume are so thoroughly oriental, so little in accordance with western thought or feeling, that they have not found an echo among ourselves. . . . The sorrows of Patient Grissel have met with sympathy in many lands, for meekness has ever been considered a womanly virtue. But the heroism of a husband and father who sells his wife to a merchant, and his son to a cowherd, in order that he may be able to keep his promise to a holy mendicant, and bestow upon him two pounds and a half of gold, can scarcely be expected to invest itself, to western eyes, with the air of a manly virtue.[3] (Ralston, in Stokes 1879, xi)*

Ralston's way of dealing with Indian folktales was the most sophisticated in a long line of similarly ambiguous positions with regard to Benfey's theory. He conceived the proposed process of diffusion of tales as one of selection by Europe. This marked his entire introduction to Stokes's volume, and many other collectors avoided an independent position. Generally, the narratives were appreciated for their aesthetic and other characteristics, but the narrators were not. Many collectors expressed surprise, like Frere, as to how "this" society could have such a narrative. Brave women of the narratives were contrasted with the oppressed among the real, folkloric kings with real monarchs, and the like. Folklore collectors' "real India" was thus rich in folklore and narrators, but backward, poor, rude, and unlearned in every other respect. The folklore collectors simultaneously regretted and welcomed the fact that the society whose lore they were collecting would vanish under their rule. This was common in their perception of different continents. Specific to India were that India was so chaotic that it was not even aware of its greatness and the folklore collector was "lifting a veil lying heavily over India's past."

The second kind of interpretation popular among colonial collectors was the attempt to trace local history through folklore. This attempt faced obvious problems, but the collectors were willing to make conclusions. In Mary Kingsley's words:

The people generally are strangely ignorant of their past, and evince very little curiosity . . . willing to leave it, and all questions dealing with the spirit-world, in the hands of their witch-doctors. . . .

To-day the whole condition of Central Africa is being metamorphosed. The country has been parcelled out among the European Powers, and in their wake, civilization is rapidly driving out barbarism and ignorance, while Christianity is infusing new life into the people, and inspiring them with noble and forceful ideas.

Fetishism is quickly dying out. . . .

Within the last ten years Toro and Bunyoro have practically swept away all outward belief in their old creeds, by gathering out from the homes of the people the charms and fetishes which were their oracle, and have publicly burned them.⁴ (vi)

Kingsley got more specific with regard to the problem of historical record among the Fjorts of West Africa who had had contact with the Roman Catholic faith through the Portuguese for many centuries. She was concerned about being able to trace the history of the people through their oral narratives, looked for the (good) influence of Christianity, and found this to be an "interesting" task:

The Roman Catholic influence over the Fjort may, I think, be taken as having been an evanescent one. . . . it suffered the common fate that has so far overtaken all kinds of attempt to Europeanise the African. It is like cutting a path in one of their native forests. You may make it a very nice path . . . it grows over again . . . . and it is his [African's] blame, not the missionary's,

> that the Fjort to-day is found by Europeans in a state of culture lower than many African tribes, and with a religion as dependent "on conversing with the Devil" as ever—in short, a very interesting person to the folklorist. (Kingsley, in Dennett 1897, xxx)

If we ignore Kingsley's obvious racist arrogance, we notice that she was pointing to the complexity of belief systems accentuated by colonialism. Maybe she was also pointing to the erosive effect of missionizing on local culture even when the "conversion" is reversed.

THEORY AND FOLKLORES OF THE EMPIRE

In 1878, when the Folk-Lore Society, London (FLS) was created, certain facts of history were important for its development. The British Empire was at its peak in Asia and Africa, and the need to understand different people was a daily necessity of the officials of the Empire. Their collective experience of establishing control was telling them that this need could best be served by knowledge of peoples' belief systems and folklore, and the collections of folklore from the colonial world had started reaching British publishers. In academia, "armchair anthropologists" James Frazer and Andrew Lang were putting forward their major theories toward the study of "primitive" people in Africa and elsewhere. The "cultures" of the British colonies were being studied not only by the British, but also by other Europeans, notably Germans, and their ideas also became important for the colonial British folklorists. Indeed, the contribution of the German scholars toward the study of Asian and African cultures in the nineteenth century was prominent, and many individual scholars and their works became standards in themselves. Max Müller was teaching in Oxford and sending out batches of officers of the Indian Civil Service with ideas of solar mythological theory in their minds. Another German whose ideas became very important for the debates of the FLS was Theodor Benfey. Benfey had suggested that India was the original homeland of all folktales—a theory which attracted the widest possible attention in Europe and elsewhere. The discussions on this theory in England at the time when India was the most important possession of Britain present very interesting sides of folklore theory and political power. It has been said that British folklore collection was also influenced by the romantic ideas coming from Germany since the beginning of the nineteenth century and the publication of a pioneering folktale collection by the Grimm brothers. While it is difficult to see any direct influence of this work on colonial folkloristics, yet it can safely be assumed to have played a role, because it had become well known throughout Europe. Even so, the colonial folklore collection was determined by its internal needs and logic. An obvious reason was the need to understand and to govern, but the officials of the Empire were also coming in contact with societies dominated by oral cultural expression and were attracted by performances, narrators, and narratives in different cultures.

The major theoretical influences on colonial folklore scholarship were of British anthropologists Andrew Lang and James G. Frazer, and German indologists Max Müller and Theodor Benfey. This division between anthropologists and philologists, including historical linguists such as Benfey, reflects aspects of the study of folklore in the colonial world: folklore was part of anthropological as well as philological concerns. In fact, we will find that both of these influences are reflected as two major trends in the writings: studying the folklore of the colonized as a sign of daily life and culture, and studying folklore as a means to learn, classify, systematize, and even develop a written script for the language of narration. The discrepancy in this accidental combination of these particular British anthropologists and German philologists is that while British anthropologists were concerned with understanding the "present" society of the colonies, the German philologists' studies were based on Indian texts in ancient Indian languages. This disjunction is not applicable in equal measure to each folklore collection, but selectively. Its major expression is in two discourses: first, in the debates of the FLS, where all four had separate supporters, and second, in many writings on Indian folklore. Indeed, at the level of theory there are significant differences in approaches to Indian and African folklore. In the following pages we will see their varied aspects.

One major difference which can be stated right away is that the philological studies, and theories based on them, formulated by Müller and Benfey applied directly only to the discussion on Indian folklore, whereas anthropologists Lang and Frazer had based their studies mainly on the study of African tribes. The discussions on African folklore remained largely within the anthropological purview; the discussions on the Indian folklore went through two phases: the earlier—in the 1870s and 1880s—dominated by different approaches, but mainly philological; and the second phase from the 1890s dominated by anthropological theories, although references to Müller's and Benfey's theories remained constant, and sometimes were used as methods of analysis. This second phase was contemporaneous with the heightened activity of folklore collection in Africa, but also influenced the analyses of Indian folklore. In other words the anthropological bent started in colonial folkloristics in 1890s and reached its high points in the first three decades of the twentieth century. Bennett offers a reason for the dominance of cultural evolution theory among British folklorists: "It was obvious how folklore fitted into this scheme. European folklore was to the history of human civilisation what the fossil record was to earth history.... Folklorists were not slow to see the significance this gave to their researches. Above all, cultural evolution gave them the opportunity to transform their 'trivial pursuit' into [at least a part of] the most exciting endeavour of the age and join the scientific community on the coat-tails of anthropology" (Bennett 1994, 29).

It is not my intention to summarize the debates in the Folk-Lore Society chronologically. A detailed summary of these debates exists in Dorson (1968) in the chapter "The Society Folklorists." I will mention here the basic positions and see their reflection in the writings of the colonial folklore collectors, with direct reference to the collections they had themselves made. Andrew Lang's position with regard to folklore was that it was the survival of another age of human culture. In *The Golden Bough* Frazer argued: "everywhere in human mental evolution a belief in magic preceded religion, which in turn was followed in the West by science. In the first stage a false causality was seen to exist between rituals and natural events. Religion appeared in the second stage, and the third stage was science. Customs deriving from earlier periods persisted as survivals into later ages, where they were frequently reinterpreted according to the dominant mode of thought." Frazer's theory placed different cultures at different points of a linear growth pattern. It thus encouraged comparative studies between societies, to understand in what relation they stood to each other in terms of evolution.

Max Müller's solar theory and comparative study of religions and languages were based on the importance of the sun and its symbolism within a culture to define how language and religions were connected to each other historically. Theodor Benfey's theory was based on the study of *Panchtantra* and its spread to Europe. Benfey argued that the majority of the tales known in the West had migrated from India. His theory made India the original homeland of folktales, and found many like-minded scholars, including M. Emanuel Cosquin and W. A. Clouston. It was a theory that received comment from the majority of the British collectors of Indian folktales. The reception of Benfey's theory by the British collectors of Indian folklore makes for an interesting study of the way colonial relations influenced the growth, popularity, and acceptance of theories of folklore.

In spite of the existence of these four positions, and the intense debates in the Folk-Lore Society, the crux of colonial folkloristics was collection, translation, and spread of the knowledge thus collected. The purpose was clear, and the need urgent. However, the point here is not simply to follow the debate, but to see how these theoretical propositions were related to the reality of the Empire. We are aware that folklore collection had as its aim better understanding and control of the subject races. We are also aware of the postcolonial critique of colonial anthropology.[5] My attempt here is to put forward the connecting moments between folklore collection and the overall theory—that factor of folklore on the basis of which the collector connects his observation with a theoretical premise. This does not mean necessary acceptance of the given theoretical premises, but also critique, rejection, and avoidance. Therefore, I will discuss the issue not chronologically, but selectively—that is, discussing a few texts that bring out the above mentioned varied aspects of colonial folklore theory.

Temple's presidential address to the Jubilee Congress of the FLS was titled "The Mind and Mental Atmosphere." The year was 1928; Temple had retired from his service in India in 1904, and he was basing his lecture on an incident of 1890. Referring to himself in the second person, as "Your President," he proposed to act neither like a guide nor "even as a teacher," but to take the audience "into his confidence and show how he has himself arrived at the theories he will describe, as that seems to be the true way for any one mind to recommend its ideas to another engaged in the same line of research." In Temple's proposal is hinted the relation between theory and praxis, that is, between colonial folklore theories and practices across the Empire. Referring to the same connection, Professor Marrett had said for Rattray, the administrator-scholar of Chinyanja and Hausa folklores of Africa:

It is our privilege at Oxford to be visited from time to time by officers of the Public Service, who modestly apply to us for instruction in Anthropology, more particularly as it bears on the history of the native races of the Empire. Not infrequently, however, they bring with them a previously acquired stock of anthropological information, such as almost takes away the breath of their duly constituted teachers. Thereupon the latter feel inclined to offer to change places; and, instead of teaching, to play the part of learners in regard to them.

Mr. Rattray furnishes a case in point. (Marrett, in Rattray 1913, v)

Indeed, many officials and missionaries from various colonies had supplied information and knowledge about different peoples, languages, lores, and cultures. The rudiments of the theory were generated in the field, not by academic researchers, but by people whose primary job was something else. In Temple's address this connection came alive as he narrated the incident on which his lecture was based and went on to build an extensive theoretical world on it: "In the early part of 1890 I was traveling by sea from Calcutta to Rangoon, being then a Government official in Burma, and, when the steamer was passing along the Arakan coast, I noticed that all the sailors on board, of whatever nationality, were performing some sort of religious ceremony in honour of something ashore. They were, as is usual in that region, a very mixed body,—Eurasians (chiefly Roman Catholic), Muslims, Hindus, Chinamen,—but, whatever they were, the ceremonies were most simple and clearly unorthodox, and were performed in the same manner by all" (Temple 1930,14). "The performance set me inquiring," said Temple (ibid.). He then went on to discuss the spread of a saint of the mariners from the Bay of Bengal to the whole of India and Persia and traced its roots back to the ancient times, connecting it with Greeks and leading on to the connections with the Christian West. At the end of this long theoretical journey, he caught up with Lang with the quotation, "What the human mind once absorbs it never lets go" (ibid., 30). Connecting his observations with Lang's abstraction, he built his theory of ancient ideas being part of the mental atmosphere of the most developed. He affirmed Frazer without mention by citing examples of belief in ghosts as the "lowliest [mental] atmosphere" (ibid., 33), being as they were at the earliest stage of human intellectual and philosophical growth.

Temple belonged to the generation before the anthropologists took over. His major works of folklore in the 1880s were concerned with documenting the versified legends and seeing in them traces of local history. Beyond that he had hoped that folklore would reveal why certain peoples are the way they are. Folklore, itself, however, was the major concern. Those were his beliefs during the early part of his career in India. What he had noticed, observed, and described—the scene on the ship—was a very "modern" visual: people of different cultures, languages, religions, and ethnicities were participating in a common ritual; it is noteworthy that this list began with "Eurasians"—people of mixed (European and Asian) descent. Unfortunately, neither Temple nor any of the armchair anthropologists who were busy studying communities-as-fixed-entities had the theoretical perspective to deal with this phenomenon—that which would be called post-modern hybridity in our times. Temple's observation does point to the fact that the folklore collector out in the colonies was witness to far more complex phenomena than the theoreticians at home could deal with, and which he himself did not have the time to ponder. After all, Temple was at the moment of his observation leading a war with Burma which brought that country under British control, and had the time to write on it only thirty-eight years later. When he saw the event he was forty years old. When he was writing on it he was seventy-eight, could not see or hear very well, had lost his family and property in England, and had handed over the treasures collected in Burma to the British Museum. He was living in a rented accommodation near a lake in Switzerland. It is remarkable that the incident was still on his mind and that he was trying to process its value for the study of folklore. With reference to Temple's "mental atmosphere" (to use his own words), senior folklorist Margaret Mills insightfully said to me that "unaccomodated data are what test and move Theory, if we are lucky and attentive" (Margaret Mills, personal communication, 2009). Temple had to take recourse in theories that could not appreciate the complexity and modernity of his materials. Like Temple, many collectors from throughout the Indian field made references to theories being formulated in Europe and took positions on them.

Rev. Charles Swynnerton, who collected folktales in the same region as Temple and around the same time—that is, in the 1880s, when Benfey's theory was dominating discussions in Europe—said of these narratives: "As folktales they claim of course the highest possible antiquity, being older than the Jâtakas, older than the Mâhabhârata, older than history itself" (Swynnerton 1892, xi). The question of age seems to be inspired by Benfey's theory. Although Swynnerton pushes back the age of his narratives even more, he is vague and at a later point in his writing clearly avoids the issue: "The question of the inter-connection which undoubtedly exists between the household tales of India and the folk-tales of other lands is one the discussion of which may be reserved for a future occasion" (Swynnerton 1892, xiii). He realizes that to many scholars "the theory of genetic relationships is the one which appears to commend itself" (ibid., xv). As regards his own position, Swynnerton retracts his steps: "The subject of the scientific value of this collection of tales I would leave to others more learned than myself" (ibid., xv). Indeed, that was an easy and discreet way out.

Rev. Knowles, who compiled a collection of Kashmiri folktales in India, also came to the subject of the diffusion of tales: "It is not my intention here to attempt to trace the home of any of these stories. Whether they originated in the East or in the West I leave to more expert and learned minds to declare" (Knowles 1888, vi). Having rightfully avoided a comment on Benfey's position since his was not a comparative exercise, he comes to Müller's theory: "much less shall I attempt to decide whether or not the root of any cycle to which these stories may belong is of a mythological nature, and also as to what was in either case its primal form and significance" (ibid., vii). He adds rather sarcastically, "Some Folk-lorists do not appear to hesitate a moment about the matter. 'It is the story of Sun and dawn,' says one" (ibid., vii). This sarcasm was born of the difference between the perceptions of men from the field and those from the armchairs. "Not long ago a writer in the *Westminster Review* startled us by duly appropriating Rájá Rasálú, who has been called the King Arthur of Panjáb, as a solar myth" (ibid., viii). Knowles was referring to a very popular figure of Punjab folklore, about whom legends had been collected by Temple and Swynnerton.

Temple, who was in the 1880s a believer of the geographical-historical school of thought, had said about this figure: "it is capable of historical proof that this man was a popular leader, on to whose name has been hung, as a convenient peg, much of the floating folk-lore of the Panjáb" (quoted in ibid., viii). Swynnerton quoted Temple's response to the writer of the article in the *Westminster Review*: "the particular tales which went to prove beyond doubt in the mind of our Comparative Mythologist that Rasálu was a solar myth, are by no means confined to that hero, but are the general property of the heroes of India, told of this one or that as occasion arises. They are, moreover, as regards Rasálu himself, to a great extent only one local version out of many of his stories" (ibid., viii). Temple's comment points to certain important aspects of folklore studies' not being taken seriously by those formulating or following over-arching theories based on a few examples. Temple's comment also reveals that he as a serious collector of folklore was aware of the larger picture, of which his collected and compiled materials were only a part, and was careful about drawing final conclusions.

Knowles also did not wish that he be seen as an opponent of comparative mythology and put forward his position: "I firmly believe that several tales must be attributed to a mythological origin. But I am also equally convinced that many tales must be attributed to a historical origin" (ibid., viii). Knowles also quoted Ralston, who believed that every "piece of evidence ought to be tested" and that any folklorist who was acquainted with a large number of tales will be less "inclined to seek for any single method of solving all their manifold problems" (ibid., ix). Ralston's argument is a convincing one. "This is the clear manifesto of data rich," commented Margaret Mills (2009).

William Crooke's presidential address to the FLS in 1911 reflected the takeover of folklore studies by anthropological theories in the early part of the twentieth century. Tracing the growth of folklore theory since the inception of the society in 1878, that is for thirty-three years, he said, "Few students of folk-tales, for instance, now believe that they are modern, or at least historical in origin; that the distinctively savage incidents embedded in them do not constitute the very core of the narrative, but are later accretions; that our European tales are derived from a single centre, whether India or any other" (Crooke 1912, 20). Crooke listed a number of "misapprehensions" related to the concerns of the folklorists and others. "Chief" of these he considered "the attempt to confuse the spheres of Comparative religion and Comparative Theology. The former aims at comparing the beliefs of savage or barbaric tribes with those current in the lower strata of civilized nations; the latter uses these facts for purposes of speculation, to refute or support the theological or dogmatic schemes of some other religion" (ibid., 19). Another misapprehension, according to him, was the vague use of the term "primitive" (ibid., 20). According to Crooke this resulted in the indiscriminate denial of solar mythology, and he was critical of it: "Though we may reasonably refuse to connect all or most of our folk-tales with the dawn or the dairy, solar myths supply the only interpretation of the Vedic and other systems, products of an advanced, not of a primitive society, and of more than one folk-tale cycle" (ibid., 21). Crooke thus placed the solar mythology theory in the context in which it was generated—Müller's study of Vedas—and pointed to another complexity, that in certain societies ancient cultural expressions may not necessarily be at any "primitive" stage. Crooke admitted that "at present" (that is, the 1910s) attention was concentrated on the study of ritual and reasoned that "the best justification of this change of method lies in the fact that, except in the esoteric cults, which form an important element in savagery, it is easier to ascertain what men do in relation to their gods, than what they think about them" (ibid., 21). Clearly, the latter would be more an area of folklore because it is born of thought and imagination. The seriousness of Crooke's comment can be understood with reference to the initial aim of folklore collection in the colonies—to understand the mind of the native.

The process of three decades of folklore collection in different colonies had also shown how difficult it was to interpret folklore in order to understand the ideas of people about themselves, their history, and their gods. Indeed, it was "easier to ascertain what men do" than to ascertain "what they think." The former was the anthropological approach, the latter required more sophisticated theoretical approaches. Crooke, though detailing different methods with a sense of fairness, himself advocated a new one, not yet much in use: "experimental psychology and the improved appliances" to understand "savage mentality" (ibid., 23). Crooke opposed Frazer's idea that magic preceded religion and stated as a counterargument that psychologists consider these "equally means to approach Divinity" without one being an "antecedent" of the other. "The services of psychology to folklore are already so considerable, that we may hope for even more important results when the field-worker and the arm-chair philosopher join forces. We owe to psychologists that interpretation of material collected in India and elsewhere which has led to the theory of Pre-animism, and seems likely to rob Animism of half its kingdom" (ibid., 25). Crooke was clearly articulating the divide that existed among the British folklore scholars: the field-worker on one side and the armchair philosopher on the other. These two needed to emerge as the composite personality of a folklorist, and perhaps Crooke carried that combination within himself, but it remained limited in expression. He knew that psychology would not be able to define the folklore studies in totality and added, "It is, however, on ethnography or ethnogeography that the future progress of our studies mainly depends" (ibid., 27).

Almost all major theoretical currents had been reflected in the study of Indian folklore, but none had an overall sway. The philological theories found an ambiguous response. Most of the collectors emphasized the antiquity of the tales they had collected, but were not willing to agree with the idea that India was the homeland of the folktale. On the other hand, the historical-geographical school did influence early works of Temple, but the obvious problems in establishing historical truth through folklore did not let the method advance very far. Temple, too, emphasized the anthropological value of folklore—as knowledge that could establish familiarity and rapport with the subject-races. In his lecture in 1928, one of the most serious writings by him, he was also pointing to the value of folklore as the collective "mental atmosphere" of people. Temple's description of the inspiring moment—a ship with sailors of different nationality led by Temple—was emblematic of an emerging world in which the ethnic identities of common people were being redefined by their changing lives. Temple's observation did not concern a romantic, pastoral community situation, but that of ordinary people of different identities on a British warship en route to Burma. But they had a common narrative—that of saint Buddhamakam—and the associated symbols. He was introducing a very modern situation of folklore and folk belief. Crooke, too, was insightful in his analysis of the theoretical approaches. He is identified as an anthropologist by latter-day social scientists, but that seems to be an underestimation of one of the best folklorists of the British colonial world. This anthropologist identification stems from the fact he never wrote about his folktale collection, nor published it. More than a century later the materials collected by him in association with Ram Gharib Chaube have been published and point toward a folklorist much ahead of his European colleagues in method and reflection.

The situation of theory in Africa is dominated by anthropological perspectives proposed by Lang and Frazer—that is, the estimation of African folklore was colored by the theories of cultural evolution, and folklore was used by default as a record of history. Already in 1968, this problem had been discussed at length by M. S. M. Kiwanuka in his article "Bunyoro and the British: A Rappraisal of the Causes for the Decline and Fall of an African Kingdom." Kiwanuka also commented on the role of John Roscoe and his associate Sir Apolo Kagwa in the history of a lost kingdom. His article brought out the involvement of a colonial folklorist in the actual history of the people whose folklore he collected. British collectors of African folklore were categorical in their estimation of historical relativity: "In any case, however, we are now some 2000 years in advance of the negro, and that is a gap which cannot be cleared at a bound" (Ellis 1890, 12). This was the benchmark for almost all shades of interpretations that established direct relationship between narratives and social organization. When collectors noticed folklore with traces of more recent histories, then they considered them unnecessary for collection and contaminations of the tradition. In a remarkable combination, tradition was simultaneously established and decried. As in Australia, the obvious question must be raised: why collect folklore when it is a sign of ways of living that would not be allowed to exist. One is not speaking here of gradual disappearance in a historical process, but of being administratively, systematically banned from practice. One is also not discussing the merits or demerits of those cases, but the underlying attitudes. The feeling of being "in control" of the situation colors all perspectives. India was comfortable, but not fathomable. Africa was under control, but uncomfortable. Indian folklore itself was a contrast to the rude and unlearned narrators, conservative society, and religious characteristics. African folklore was an exact replica of her people. As the British collectors confronted cultures where cultural expression was solely oral, the collection of folklore was part of developing scripts for the language concerned. This per se was pioneering activity and is the reason for granting major credit to the collectors of African folklore. This credit, too, issues from the belief that the written word is higher in cultural history than orality—a concept now more or less universal, except among ethnographers of literacy and folklorists. The conversion of oral lore into written thus has dimensions in certain colonies not necessarily shared by others.

Philological studies were more the pioneering attempts at evolving written languages out of the oral ones. The discussion on tales, therefore, had more reference to classification and interpretation. There were few, if any, comments on the relation of African tales with those of other continents. Smith and Dale claimed that "Africa is the home of animal tales. Was not the greatest fabulist of all an African?—the famous Lokman to whom Mohammed inscribed the 31st Sura of the Koran, and whom the Greeks, not knowing his real name, called Aesop, i.e. Ethiops? Be that as it may, we can claim the stories of Uncle Remus as African in origin; they were taken by the slaves across to America . . ." (Smith and Dale 1920, 342). Even so, Browne, like many others, dwelt only on the connection of African tales with other African tales:

> *The persistence of the same incidents in tales coming from such widely separate African tribes is not to be accounted for by any hypothesis of borrowing, but seems to point to the fact that before the Bantu migrated from their original home in the north, they already possessed these tales. If that is so, we are dealing with things not of yesterday, but of two or three thousand years ago. That would not, of course, apply to all the tales, many of them may be quite modern. The day will come perhaps, when by comparing such collections of tales from different parts of the field, we shall be able to get some idea which are ancient. (Smith and Dale 1920, 342–43)*

The theoretical approach to the African folklore justifies Bennett's comment that the colonial folkloristics was largely dominated by one perspective: "Almost since the inception of the Folklore Society (FLS) in 1878, folkloristic concepts and methods have been dominated by a single theory of culture—'cultural evolution' (alternatively called 'social evolution' or 'sociocultural evolution')" (Bennett 1994, 25). African tales got investigated for historical points of origin for tales, but not for historical content per se.

I have shown that the anthropological perspective was not the only one, but its dominance in the later phase of colonial folkloristics cannot be denied. The theories regarding the folklores from the colonies of the British Empire were formulated exclusively by the British collectors. Although underlying principles were the same in different collections, yet the difference with regard to the perceived relationship of African and Indian folklore texts to others is remarkable. While Indian folklore is shown to be related with many others, African folklore is conceptually isolated, studied with reference to itself, and interpreted freely with reference to the collectors' values.

There is another interesting aspect of colonial folklore theory: that it compared folklore of different colonies with the European, but did not compare the folklore of different colonies with each other. No colonial scholar sought to establish links between Indian and African folklore. This absence reveals a crucial aspect of colonial folklore scholarship: it saw every movement as *either to or from* Britain. By their study of the colonies and distribution of their writings they were creating new loops of cultural networks, but each one of those loops was connected to Britain.

CONCLUSION

The colonial folklore scholarship was neither without theoretical perspective nor without the attempt to theorize upon the materials. The collectors tried to interpret, classify, and theoretically evaluate the folklore they collected. By the analysis of the fragments of theoretical formulations, the constants and variables of the colonial folklore scholarship emerge clearly. The "constant" was the belief that folklore reveals the mind of its carriers. The variable was the individual capacities of the colonial collectors to present theoretical formulations. Some were capable of and did present their ideas to their contemporaries. At this stage we encounter another factor, that this scholarship was literally spread over many continents. Not only were the collections published in Britain, but the collector too had to gain his identity in Britain. Here, however, he was confronted by the full-time scholars and university academics whose ideas about peoples they had never encountered dominated the discourses in England. Although this power struggle is not recorded anywhere, except in some oblique comments by William Crooke, yet its evidences are many. Almost all the scholars whose theoretical influences have been cited and assumed had never actually been in the locales of culture they were theorizing about. The collectors often found acceptance in the scholarly communities, but were seen more as knowledgeable about the empirical realities of the few places they had lived in, rather than as theorists themselves.

The importance of the writings of the collectors is in the details of their writing where theoretical principles are juxtaposed to specific empirical phenomena and theoretical formulations arise from the perception of empirical realities. That is, indeed, the process in which folklore theory should emerge. That is why I have attempted here to cull the theoretical perspectives of the colonial folklore collectors from their writings on folklore. These should be the basis of our contemporary perception of colonial folkloristics as folklore theory. Herein we see that it is not only not an offshoot of European folkloristics, but also an attempt to rise over the provincial nature of European folkloristics. Colonial folklore theory reflects all biases that the colonizers are known to have had about the colonized—religious, social, political, moral, and intellectual. Yet, beyond its ideology it is a theory that deals with international, intercultural, and multilingual aspects of folkloristics as a transnational discipline. The theoretical implications of colonial folkloristics were the following:

1. A folklorist does not have to belong to the community whose folklore she or he is documenting; she or he does not have to know the language of narration and performance. To get past these hurdles she or he has to work toward executing a plan in which translators are an important consideration.
2. Folklorists become scholars in the process of constructing and interpreting the translated English texts. In colonial folklore theory this transformation of the administrators into folklore-scholars is as important as the transformation of the folklores into English language texts. The folklores become international texts and the folklorists become international scholars. The international identity of the tales is expressed in texts as well as in publications that travel around the world. The international identity of the folklorists is evidenced in the recognition granted to them by their peers and states, and in their status as scholars in postcolonial folkloristics.
3. In colonial folklore theory, unlike European romantic folklore theory, the folk is not expected to be sanitized and made dearer to the middle-class imagination. The colonized folk must appear extremely exotic, wild (not natural), generally cruel, superstitious, cunning (not intelligent), and certainly "untouched by European civilization." This image is meant to shock or amuse the readers. With reference to the popular ideology of Victorian morality, the colonized folk appeared to be amoral and immoral.
4. Throughout the colonial writings some factors are consistently missing: signs of colonial stress on the colonized, narratives about the British, and resistance to colonial rule. The consistency with which these factors are missing points to the fact that colonial folkloristic theory was a highly conscious expression. This consistency, in the context of the size of the Empire and the distance between collectors, is amazing. It may be rooted in the ideologies ingrained in the collectors' minds before they left the

United Kingdom, or were accepted in colonial service—because their ideas are commensurate with its premises.
5. Another feature of colonial folkloristics is a clear disdain, if not hatred, for the religious beliefs of the narrators in most of the cases, and in others no appreciation for them. This is equally true of missionaries and others.
6. In spite of the dominance of empirical observations, the folklorist does not need to specify the specific place and time of collection. These are mentioned in very broad terms.
7. In colonial folkloristics it is perfectly acceptable that the folklorist does not pay any heed to the classification systems and interpretations of the narrators themselves.
8. Indeed, interpretation of the narratives is the most important task of the folklorist, and the interpretation can be completely unrelated to the interpretations of the narrators and their audience. In the interpretations history, anthropology, and psychology are entwined with each other. These entwined strands are colored by the overall ideology of colonialism. This overall ideology of colonialism has been defined by scholars from different postcolonial contexts: Latin American scholar Walter Mignolo sees it as a combination of race, violence, and power and terms it coloniality of power; African philosopher V. Y. Mudimbe terms the combination of scientific and ideological discourse on Africa as African *gnosis*: "It is the *episteme* of the nineteenth and early twentieth centuries that invented the concept of a static and pre-historic tradition. Travelers' reports localize African cultures as 'beings-in-themselves' inherently incapable of living as 'beings-for-themselves'" (Mudimbe 1988, 189). Foucault's proposition that the entire history of the human sciences from the nineteenth century onward can be retraced on the basis of three conceptual pairs, *function and norm, conflict and rule,* and *signification and system,* is particularly relevant to us. We can see that all three pairs appear in colonial folkloristics: function of the norms of colonized peoples; the conflict of interests and the rule of the colonizer; and most importantly folklore as historical, psychological, and anthropological signification of society and therefore a system through which people can be known.

If we apply these theses about the production of colonial knowledge bodies to colonial folklore collections, how would we categorize colonial folklore theory? My answer to this question is that colonial folklore theory was not only a part of the overall colonial knowledge, but it was the location where colonial culture theory was articulated. The quintessential difference between the colonizer and the colonized was identified in "writing" and "orality," respectively. From the projection of this difference resulted the corresponding hierarchy between writing and orality. Colonial folklore theory was *the* culture theory of the British Empire.

CHAPTER 5

The Story-Time of the British Empire
Transnational Folkloristics as Theory of Cultural Disjunctions

> In a country where darkness reigns as soon as the lamp of the sun goes down,
> the story, told around the fire at night, takes the place of the arm-chair book
> in the brilliantly-lighted home.
> DOKE 1927, XV

Analyses of motives, methods, and interpretations of the British collectors of Indian and African folklore allow for certain generalizations to emerge. The "global" situation of the colonial folkloristics was at one level only conceptual. For individual collectors it was limited to their engagement with folklore of one or two colonies. Many collectors compiled only a single volume of folklore collection, while some wrote more, but on one or two regions or communities. The narrators, too, were narrating in their "age-old" locales. So how was the situation global? What does "global" mean in this context and how did it impact the growth of an international discipline? In the preceding four chapters of this book we have discussed the facts of this global situation. In this chapter I try to show how those facts are connected with many current aspects of the discipline of folkloristics, and it is in this that the relevance of the present study can be seen. Intellectual paradigms emerge in particular socio-political contexts, but continue to exist and function beyond those contexts. Accordingly, the influence of the long and active phase of folklore scholarship in the colonial British Empire can be seen on current folklore theories and on the public and academic status of folklore in the erstwhile colonies. So, in this chapter I will discuss how the situation of colonial British folklore collectors was global and how it impacted the future of the discipline and of several performative practices.

First, the situation of colonial folkloristics was global because the consciousness of the colonial collectors was global. They were conscious and aware of their nation's Empire in different parts of the world and were conscious of their colleagues in other locales. They knew that the bit role they were playing in representing a people was as big as that people and their place in the Empire. Unlike the nationalist folklore collectors of Europe, the aims of colonial collectors were not so localized and narrow as the change of a political regime or even a system. The aims of the colonial collectors were to create the *first ever* sketches of different peoples of the world, and folklore was the pencil and color with which they drew and painted. They were not collecting folklore to uphold native values, but so as to be able to replace them with the so-called modern ones. They were aware that the modern values were also "foreign" values for the field of their folklore collection, but indeed their designated job was to usher in this modernity.

Second, the situation was global because similar methods and theoretical concepts were applied to a vast variety of folklore systems in the world. This has affected the development of folkloristics in a particular manner. The colonial collectors sought the same genres that they knew from home, all across the world. Rarely are the native categories for narratives mentioned. They did not define, categorize, and analyze the narratives of different cultures and continents with their own terms of reference. This led to the few generic terms being applied to narratives even vaguely similar to those known in the collector's culture. For example, "ballad" was applied to a variety of narrative songs in northern India instead of also documenting and using categories that existed for them and reflected their different aesthetic and thematic nuances. This means that identification of folklore genres of the erstwhile colonized cultures needs to be undertaken again, instead of the widespread tendency of using the existing genre names with broad implications. It also means that a *theoretical* obliteration of many genres of the folklore of the colonized started much before their *physical* obliteration. This matter is of much significance because once the records were drawn they gained the sanctity of written records, and the postcolonials have sometimes deployed them to fight for their "traditional" rights. For example, George Abraham Grierson, who conducted a massive linguistic survey of India in the last decade of the nineteenth century, has in recent years been criticized for his division of Indian languages and dialects and the kind of linguistic politics it has unleashed in postcolonial India. And yet, the status of Grierson's work is such that even a small linguistic community can claim its legal rights by citing the mention that their language received in Grierson's record. This is applicable in folklore research in another manner—some regions and folklore were researched or documented by many collectors while others were not.

Beyond the socio-political implications, this method also hampered the enrichment that folkloristics could have experienced in terms of categories of genres and knowledge about them. The method of colonial collectors, which seems haphazard, ad hoc, and gathered along the way, is also an expression of the variety of "folklores" and their even more varied statuses in different societies. It is the evidence of the heterogeneity of locales, narrators, narratives, and collectors. In some places the narratives constituted precepts for social and personal conduct and had the authority to demand compliance; in some other places the narratives seemed like coded history; in yet other locales narration and narratives were woven into the daily life of the community; and yet elsewhere the customary and ritualistic need for the narratives secured their survival. The colonial collectors' method is not without the influence of these realities, but these men and women were witnesses to phenomena they were not intellectually prepared to comprehend.

This incomprehension has remained couched under a few theoretical concepts applied to varied realities. Theories of the armchair scholars in England actually hampered a clearer view for the men of the field. We see sudden glimmers of understanding and insight in the writings of some collectors that remain unsubstantiated by theoretical abstraction. Smith and Dale say for the narratives in *The Ila-Speaking People of Northern Rhodesia*: "To us there is a lack of coherence in many of the details and explicit contradictions pull us up and spoil our pleasure, as when Fulwe, after being cooked and eaten, gives Sulwe his doom. But such things do not annoy the Ba-ila or detract from their enjoyment. For one thing Fulwe, though dead, lives in his race; it is a mere accident that one individual dies; it is the ideal Fulwe, not the Fulwe who merely breathes, but the Fulwe in the narrator's mind, and he is immortal" (Smith and Dale 1920, 344).

In this observation on the life and death of a fictional character, Smith and Dale were pointing to a crucial philosophical perception as expressed through the narratives—the idea of self, the idea of individual existence, and the relationship between the "ideal" and the life and death of an individual. This is a subject concerned with African philosophy that the collectors did not elaborate upon, but they did highlight the subject of "mentality" as reflected in the folklore.

Ghanian philosopher Kwame Gyekye (1988) says that the African concepts of the individual and self are always in a relation of subservience to the social organization. Kenyan theology professor John S. Mbiti (1969) articulates African philosophy thus: "Whatever happens to the individual happens to the whole group, and whatever happens to the whole group happens to the individual. The individual can only say: 'I am, because we are; and since we are, therefore I am.' This is a cardinal point in the understanding of the African view of man" (1969, 109). Smith and Dale were close to noticing this quintessential difference from "I think, therefore I am" and/or from European ideas of individualism, but they did not ponder long enough and reach what they and their colleagues claimed to have set out to do—namely, to decode the ideas of the people. Their observation glimmers within a text that otherwise upholds the colonial paradigm of understanding the colonized as "primitive." Crooke was right in pointing out the confusion arising from the incorrect and vague use of the term "primitive," but was unable to offer an equivalent concept to this hugely successful one. The open secret of the success of the term "primitive" was that it could bind the cultures of the Empire in a vertical hierarchy that corresponded with the political, military, and economic structures. Primitive as different from civilized could be read as colonized as different from the colonizer; and above all, the difference could be read as the difference between "orality" and "writing." Graham Furniss has discussed different academic approaches to orality, and pointed out—on the basis of examples from different cultures—how the notions related with orality as pre-industrial, rural, and constantly changing do not exactly apply to various forms of oral communication. Folklorists are aware that many folklore genres are *oral and stable* in their composition—for example, oral epics. Furniss points out that the hierarchy between orality and writing did not exist in ancient Greek discourse, or else the importance given to rhetoric would have been absent. So, when does this hierarchy of orality's being inferior to writing emerge? One such hierarchy emerges in the colonial context, and reflects other forms of hierarchies as well.

This hierarchy finds another parallel in the power structures of colonial folkloristics. At first glance, it may seem to be a false conflict, but it is still remarkable that leaders in the field of theory were armchair anthropologists and philologists in universities in England who were developing their concepts on the basis of the materials collected by missionaries and administrators. The men of the field had a secondary status within the scholarly circles at home. Although honored by awards and doctorates, yet their situation became akin to that of their native associates: materials were expected from them, but not theory. A couple of theoretical approaches developed in England were used to conceptualize almost a quarter billion people. This is certainly an important characteristic of the colonial model of folkloristics—that while it lacked the intellectual capability to comprehend the diversity of the multitudes of folklores, it applied a few theoretical concepts en masse. Additionally, through these concepts they participated in the ideology of the imperial states, and through folklore articulated a vision that would not rock the colonial state.

Third, colonial folkloristics was global because its materials came from different cultures and the publications had the whole world to travel to, even if they just followed the same network all the way back to the "colony" they came from. Actually, the travel was already so wide that collections of folklore of one colony were not retailed in other colonies (except in the personal libraries of British residents). Even today, in the twenty-first century, it would be difficult to find R. S. Rattray's collections of African folklore in an Indian library, not to speak of their (un)availability in the retail book market. Similarly, it would be equally difficult to find William Crooke's books in Africa. It was certainly impossible that Pandit Chaube could know his contemporary Malam Shahiu, and they remain unknown to their own future generations, not to speak of being known in each other's societies. And the incongruities do not end here: Rattray, Crooke, and their colleagues like Temple and Dennett may not have gained the status of theorists in British folkloristics, but in South Asia and Africa they are seen as pioneer theorists of the folk culture of the countries where they compiled their volumes of books. On the obverse side of the same logic, all of them can be found in the libraries of the "western" world.

The incongruities are poignant, and yet, these should not cloud our vision and lead us to a critique based on binary oppositions, not only because the binary oppositions can only be theoretical, but also because such critique would be undermined by postcolonial realities. We need to see and state that probably the biggest contribution of colonial folklore studies is the development of a transnational folkloristics whose methods and interpretative categories could be applied to different locales. As argued earlier, their avoidance of local classificatory categories deprived folkloristics of possible enrichment, but their application of European categories filled those categories with a wide variety of materials and subverted their original European-ethnological meanings (*volkskundliche Bedeutung*en). In spite of the change of ideologies, their methods continue to be followed by scholars researching in intercultural, international, and multilingual contexts. Folklore educational institutions in the United States often have specialists on different geographic regions of the world, in Germany Volkskunde and Völkerkunde distinguish European and non-European folklore studies, in Britain Asian and African studies exist as separate fields of study within which folklore is included. In South Asia and

Africa the focus of folklore studies remains on self. Colonial folkloristics created and has left behind a rich field for the emergence of new approaches in comparative studies, gender perspective, tale-type categorizations, translation studies, and postcolonial theory. The shortcomings of the colonial folkloristics have remained because of the absence of postcolonial analytical engagement with these works, but in the very critique of colonial folkloristics are the seeds for a more advanced and democratic international folkloristics.

Writing from across the Empire, British colonial folklorists drafted a folklore map of the world. This map showed two things: one, what kinds of folklore existed across the Empire; and two, that these were all linked to each other in a global history of culture. The first aspect of this map painted an Empire very rich in folklore of different varieties and languages. There were oral narratives and songs all around the world, and what the colonial folklore collectors were witnessing and experiencing was definitely beyond the scope of what in Europe had been termed folklore, folktale, folksong, and the like. This map could redefine the image of folktale beyond the conceptions of European folkloristics. Folktale was not just a form of entertainment of rural groups, but was found performing different roles in different societies. These roles were not necessarily religious or ritualistic, but of more complex natures. Indeed, only some of the roles of storytelling were universal, such as the role in children's informal education, but there were many roles that the folktale performed that were not known to European folkloristics. This colonial map of folklore was also plentifully stocked with professional and casual storytellers. There were communities of storytellers. Narratives and narrators had different kinds of status in the societies concerned; they were integrated in the economic and cultural structures of their societies.

Perhaps no European collector within his home country would have encountered such a vast number of "problems" as were faced by the collectors in the colonies, nor did they have the privileges of power enjoyed by the colonial collectors. Although many aspired to compile scholarly collections, and in some sense of the word did compile them, yet their own "mental atmosphere," to use Temple's term, as administrators did not allow for free theoretical evaluation, or as missionaries did not allow them to rise above their religious biases, or as women to rise above the boundaries of intellectual complacency. They could not but see folklore of other cultures in comparison to their own. The model of colonial folkloristics is a contemporary of the early European folkloristics, but it is an independent model of folklore collection, research, and study. It is neither an offshoot of the European folkloristics, nor essentially similar to it.

POLITICS OF COLONIAL FOLKLORISTICS

Through the nineteenth century and the first half of the twentieth century, the politics of the folklore collectors can be divided into two categories that encompass in themselves many ideologies:

1. The folklore collectors that were against the state or powers that were—folklorists who saw their act of the transformation of the oral narrative expression of the common folk as a means to culturally, intellectually, aesthetically, and/or politically empower the same sections.
2. Those who were on the side of the state or the powers that were—folklorists who compiled oral cultural expression into written volumes to create various aspects of the identity of the state itself and make folklore a symbol and definition of society in the manner the state would like to represent it.

Colonial folkloristics presents a case of close relationship between the state and folklore collectors. As we have seen, the colonial collectors were directly or indirectly representatives of the colonial state, in their own eyes and in those of their narrators. Their writings, which have been considered lacking in theory, show that the theoretical perspectives of a folklore collector are born not only of consciously chosen paradigms, but also of his or her objective relationship with the state. As such, relationship with political ideologies of the time is suggested. Indeed, colonial folklore collectors are not the only ones with a political view—political consciousness is the very starting point of folklore studies. Therefore, it is important to understand how the political ideology of the colonial folklore collectors differed in essence from that of others.

The politics of colonial folklorists is at one level clear because they were representatives of the colonial state. From Mary Frere to Mary Kingsley, and from Richard Carnac Temple to Robert Sutherland Rattray, all collectors were extremely conscious of their individual position and of their state's power. They were the personification of that power. More important, none of them had any essential difference of opinion with the policies of the state and thus identified with the state. Some of them, like Crooke, were critical of the administrative policies, but none ever expressed any doubt over the very existence of their rule over other people. Indeed, they did not even see the "evils" of colonial rule with regard to folklore.

At another level, however, their politics generated a kind of folklore scholarship whereby oral lore of peoples was used to define them against their own interests. And although such scholarship interpreted a lot from the texts collected, it rarely treated the narrators as sources of knowledge. Very few of the collectors I have mentioned even identified the narrators by name. When they did it was in a fashion that kept them not really visible. Only in Crooke's collection were the names systematically written above the texts. In Torrend's collection of Bantu folklore (1921), the name appears at the end of each text, most often in the first person, "I am MWANA RUMINA," "I am CIBUTA," etc. (Torrend 1921, 12, 17), because Torrend made phonographic recordings. Torrend writes a few words about their identities in the footnotes, which are very interesting and reveal that a large number of narrators were regular visitors or members of the Kasisi Mission in Northern Rhodesia. This kind of information was not the norm, and generally narrators were not mentioned. As such the colonial scholarship disconnected the colonized from their knowledge resources. On the other hand, the folklore collector with his interpretations took on the mantle of the historian. Interestingly, history has emerged as a major discipline of study in Africa. Until the 1960s the historian in Africa was a collector and translator of oral sources; since the 1990s this school of history writing has been seen as "silencing the African voice" (White et al. 2002) and newer ways of studying oral expression toward an understanding of history have been proposed.

Across the world, perspectives of folklore collectors toward the state have played different and very important roles in their act of textualizing orality. The role of the Grimms' folktale collection in the construction of the idea of nation is a well-discussed theme. Another interesting example, and here suitably comparable, is the role of Elias Lonrott—native folklorist of a colonized country, Finland. He gave his colonized people a whole new identity to be proud of. The colonial British collectors of folklores objectified the folk and lore of Asia and Africa for Europe. Their politics was not on a national scale, but transnational. As such, it was far more futuristic than nationalist folklore scholarship. It created intellectual and political loops of international cultural network in which the oral expressive cultures of the erstwhile colonized peoples and their study is still trapped.

COLONIAL FOLKLORISTICS, TRADITION, AND MODERNITY

One of the related contributions of the colonial folkloristics has been use of the term "traditional" as in opposition to "modern." Colonial folklore collectors identified folklore as "traditional" narrative and poetic expression of the peoples of the colonies. "Tradition" implied practices and perspectives were static, unchanging, unrelenting, unrequired, undesired, and just a matter of habit, a trope that has been seriously critiqued and revised in the twentieth century (Hobabawm and Ranger 1983, Bauman and Briggs 2003). "Modern" for the colonies meant "western" (rather, "British") values, trade, and politics, a trope still being contested. The requirement and desire for this modernity was unquestionable in the mind of the collector. Although the folklore collectors were not the only propagators of this split, yet this split characterizes the perception of culture *in* and *about* all postcolonial societies today. "In contemporary Africa one meets highly westernized and rational minds who sincerely submit to and enjoy the meaning of their mythological narratives. Each time I have used this case in public I have had to face a question from well-intentioned Westerners wondering whether those people had really assimilated the scientific habits of mind" (Mudimbe 1991, 97).

Postcolonial theorists all across the erstwhile colonized world seek to explain such complexities, and this explanation is the very subject of one of the latest works by eminent postcolonial theorist Dipesh Chakraborty. In *Provincializing Europe* (2000), he tells us how the legacy of European enlightenment ideas is a part of the day-to-day life of postcolonial Indians. While the argument makes sense at an overall level, yet it is too utopian in its formulation. Chakraborty's experience is based in Calcutta, a city established by the British, and thus the intermingling of ideas seems to be smooth. In contrast to Chakraborty's experience of Calcutta, the city of Lucknow, which was the center of the Revolt of 1857, constantly reminds a postcolonial observer that this transition of European ideas into non-European spaces was achieved through bitter power struggle. The physical realities and the ideas constantly remind the subject of the resistance, loss, and defeat.

On the plane of reality, the split is most visible in the public sphere—modern is western and indigenous is traditional. "Modernity" needs to be aspired to and tradition needs to be selectively preserved. Classified as tradition, the subject can be put in a niche, paid lip service to, presented in state festivals, but otherwise forgotten, because it is not part of the dynamism of the modern. Or, it lacks the dynamism to be modern. Foucault says: "Take the notion of tradition: it is intended to give a special temporal status to a group of phenomena that are both successive and identical (or at least similar); it makes it possible to rethink the dispersion of history in the form of the same; it allows a reduction of the difference proper to every beginning, in order to pursue without discontinuity the endless search for the origin; tradition enables us to isolate the new against a backdrop of permanence" (1972, 6). These meanings have become associated with entire erstwhile colonized peoples and cultures. It is a schizophrenic split between "traditional" and "modern" culture that is the "common wealth" of the postcolonial societies of the British Empire. And yet, this split is rarely seen as based in colonialism, or more specifically as created through the works of colonial folklore collectors. In the last two decades of the twentieth century American folklorists have offered different theoretical perspectives on studying folklore texts in socio-political contexts and seeing them as highly stylized forms of communication, in which people play a significant role as agents of perspectives of society expressed through their narratives and songs (Furniss and Gunner 1995, 1–2). In Furniss and Gunner's 1995 edited volume *Power, Marginality and African Oral Literature* there are seventeen articles that study folklore in different postcolonial African societies "not merely as folksy, domestic entertainment, but as a domain in which individuals in a variety of social roles articulate a commentary upon power relations in society and indeed create knowledge about society" (ibid., 1). The writers are distancing themselves from the colonial perceptions of folklore but do not analyze or even mention those works. In yet another anthology of articles, *Studies in Hausa Language and Linguistics* (Furniss and Jagger 1988), the work of Rattray and Malam Shaihu does not find a mention even in the bibliography. In contrast to these, Rattray and Shaihu are the heroes on the official website of the Republic of Ghana. These contradictions point to the fact that postcolonial theory has yet to have its influence outside the academy, where the notions created in colonial times continue to be popular and often used by now-independent states to further their own agenda. Indeed, such agendas may be existent in an "independent" nation, but carry an intellectual continuity. The contribution of South Asian scholars in the articulation of postcolonial theory is well-known, but none of those theoretical writings have analyzed colonial folklore collections. And thus, colonial collectors and collections continue to retain their status for academic and nonacademic purposes.

Folklore and folk performers are constantly used in the construction of national cultural identity by the state in its ceremonies and festive occasions, but also continue to remain outside of educational curricula of schools and colleges. As sociological phenomena, what exists is the continuous but unpredictable mingling of the two—tradition and modernity. Their cultures today can best be described as "hybrid." James Lassiter discusses this in the context of Africa and mentality studies:

During the late 1950s and 1960s, national character and typical personality studies were broadly condemned, breathed their last gasp, and were ultimately relegated to the dustbin of bad social science. Since that time, various African scholars outside the social sciences have nevertheless been sustaining and redirecting group personality inquiry. They are not, however, approaching their subject as did Western social scientists in the first half of this century who used questionnaire instruments to determine if Africans were "traditional" or "modern." . . . They did this, for the most part, to find out which African groups were better suited for white or blue collar work in the colonial and post-independence socioeconomic setup. . . .

African scholars writing on these subjects since the early 1960s have taken a humanistic, liberating or empowering approach. . . . For example, the work of University of Nairobi philosophy professor Joseph M. Nyasani (1997) . . . is a recent attempt to define the "African psyche." (Lassiter 1999)

Nyasani (1997, 56–57) sees African, Asian, and European minds as conditioned by their different environments and age-old cultural systems, and therefore different from each other. As Lassiter points out, twentieth-century African scholars have conducted the discourse with new aims, yet the discourse itself was initiated in the colonial context, and by folklore collectors.

Garcia Canclini offers many insights into the conflict between tradition and modernity in the formerly colonized societies. His study of Latin American countries, especially Mexico, presents a situation recognizable in Asia and Africa, too, "where tradition has not yet disappeared and modernity has not completely arrived" (Canclini 1995, 1). The processes of "entering" and "exiting" modernity in postcolonial societies is intricately linked with their colonial legacies and the definitions of the cultures of the "original" inhabitants of these countries. The postcolonial theoretical perspective has analyzed and presented the cultural complexity of these societies in current times, and the post-modern theoretical perspective analyzes the disjunctions in the current cultural mosaic of the developed countries. Are these two different situations? Or, are the differences two sides of the same coin? I would like to proceed with the latter assumption. The confrontationist debate between "tradition" and "modernity" implies that these two strains exist exclusively of each other in culture. This is not the ground reality. Cancilini's theory of "hybridity" in cultural life of modern nations is well known. This hybridity, however, is not only the result of a historical process, but was also partially willed by the colonial culture theorists. Henry Balfour, president of the Folk-Lore Society, advocated in 1923 a process of "gradual" change in the mentality of the "primitive" people across the Empire. "To root up old established indigenous trees and plant alien substitutes to which the soil is unsuited is a useless and unproductive exercise.... But, while cutting down of a vigorous and deeply-rooted stem causes the death of the plant and all that depends on its vitality, judicious pruning may be quite feasible; and moreover, it should be possible to graft branches of a different nature quietly upon it, and to repeat the process, until the whole nature of the growth has changed without loss of vitality" (Balfour 1923, 17, 23).

Since the mid-twentieth century, increasing numbers of folklore scholars, and not administrators, missionaries, and traders, have traveled to other linguistic and cultural zones to collect folklore. Issues of language and cultures have been ever present, too. At times they have known the language of the folklore concerned, and at other times not. At times they have been students of the larger cultural context of the folklore concerned, and at other times not. At times they have transcribed the local language alongside the language of the book concerned, at other times not. Have they published the texts in the local languages themselves? No, they have not. The language of the publication continues to be the language of the collector and the region of his birth and employment, and of publishing, especially.

Change has been most visible in the intercultural perceptions, although the difference between "tradition" and "modern" has continued. With the independence movements and freedoms gained from the British colonial rule, a reevaluation and increasingly bitter critique of "colonial" perceptions have been the germination ground of many new perspectives. At an overall level, establishing direct and large-scale connections between the folklore, sociology, and history of the narrators has been given up in favor of broadly cultural-relativist and liberal ideas. Folklorists have tried to see the "other" culture behind the folklore they collected in more conscious, informed, and nonjudgmental ways. The overarching concern has been with the materials of folklore and internationally applicable approaches to their study. The discussion on the ideological contents of folklore has been guarded and with reference to strictly defined contexts.

Interpretations have been guided by approaches within the discipline, and also by philosophical and ideological waves coming from other disciplines. Folkloristics today is indeed one of the most international disciplines in the humanities, probably next only to the natural sciences, with regard to its methods, materials, scholars, applicability of interpretations, institutions, and connectivity between these. It is a discipline that deals in micro-level specifics of cultural expression and finds universal parallels and interested readers, even though not often by the same folklorist. The world of folklore has been without boundaries since ever, and the world of folklorists and folkloristics has been global since the mid-nineteenth century. In this increasingly global world, this international identity is not only a gain, but a factor that has the potential of making the discipline relevant to students of cultures. Colonial folkloristics was the starting point of this international identity, and the precursor of the present and the future of folklore studies.

"Post-modernity" is an experience of disjunctions, and a post-modern folkloristics needs disciplinary disjunctions. A folklore scholar needs to be a "nomad," like Canclini, between the disciplines separated from each other with industrial cleanliness. The truth behind the practice of folklore even in the remotest village of a country like India is not simple, but complex.

In the on-the-ground reality of folklore scholarship, folklorists and narrators are subject to various power structures, some of them in line with the colonial experiences, while others are of a new kind. The examples on the surface are the lack of infrastructure for the study of folklore in the postcolonial societies. With reference to the contemporary international movement of folklore scholars, this study of the colonial folkloristics encourages us to pick up at least one aspect for discussion: namely, the interculturality in contemporary folklore scholarship. The decidedly international nature of folklore studies today is also intercultural and needs analysis. There is no hiding from this issue behind the theories of textualization and archiving, and one needs to analyze how interculturality is influencing the folklore scholarship. It exists not only between folklorists from the developed world and narrators from the developing, but also when scholars of developing countries study the folklore theories in the institutions of the developed world, then return like visiting scholars to "collect" materials from the fields in India, Africa, and the like. Though no computation is available, it can safely be said that even today works on Indian or African folklore by "western" scholars will outnumber many times over those done by Indian or African scholars. There are very few South Asian or African folklorists who research European folklore. To an extent, these are the legacies of colonial folkloristics.

There is probably no other model of folkloristics[1] as the British colonial version which was generated in so many cultures across the globe in an almost parallel manner and wherein collectors are exclusively from one culture studying all others. This is not comparable to the "international" reach of a folklore collection or international influence of pioneers like the Brothers Grimm. Colonial folkloristics is about the existence of a vast body of folklore collections that were inherently international and intercultural in their scope and influence. The importance of these characteristics is not only for our conceptualization of colonial folkloristics but also for reconsidering some of our current perceptions.

Colonial folkloristics is a global theory of disjunctions. It completely negates Herder's notion of folklore as the unity of language, spirit, and nation. Its point of departure is a historical series of experiences of disjunction. To begin with, the collector is physically disconnected from his own language and nation. Then he becomes the representative of the forces causing disjunctions in the societies of the colonized. The narrators are experiencing quintessential changes in the performance context of their oral texts, and get to perform in unprecedented contexts (for example, before a foreigner collector who, they know, does not understand what they are narrating). Performers also know that this time their narration is for a written record, but they have no control over it. The text gets textualized and printed in another language, in another country, for a readership that can almost not imagine the narrators who narrated the texts. This published text, temporally and spiritually disconnected from the narrators, becomes the definition of the narrators and their societies.

And finally, the time of storytelling: colonial folklore collections tell us that the most preferred time of storytelling—pure narrative performance—was the evening, when the sun had gone down and the narrators and their audience were lit from above by night sky and from below by the light of a fire. The printed text matched the scale of the Empire: it could be read simultaneously across the globe in different time zones and therefore at different times of the day for different recipients—*"for readers of ease and culture whether in the East or in the West,"* as Swynnerton said (1892, vi). The story-time of the British Empire was *all* the time.

Colonialism created cultural disjunctions, and colonial folkloristics became the record, the evidence, and an agent of these disjunctions. As such, colonial folkloristics is the harbinger of postcolonial and post-modern culture theories that take cognizance of pluralities in perspectives, layers in sociocultural phenomena, and transnational identities. Colonial folkloristics should be seen as a record and theory of colonial cultural disjunctions that conjoin with postcolonial and post-modern realities.

NOTES

CHAPTER 1. FIELDS

1. The dominance of this perspective in folklore studies has remained in spite of theories in other fields of the humanities that have challenged the legitimacy of Eurocentric perspectives. Benedict Anderson's *Imagined Communities* (1991) placed the emergence of nation states in Europe within larger contexts of world politics. Walter Mignolo has shown in his *Local Histories/Global Designs* (2000) how "modernity" was not fabricated in Europe and exported to the colonized countries, but that modernity itself emerged in the context of colonialism and associated relations of race, power, and violence. Bauman and Briggs (2003) have analyzed the emergence of the notion of "modernity" as opposed to "tradition" in seventeenth- and eighteenth-century England, and in eighteenth- and nineteenth-century Germany; their discussion shows how the discourse of modernity objectified and marginalized "tradition" simultaneously. Briggs and Naithani (forthcoming) have argued that acceptance of a Eurocentric paradigm in folklore theory is a sign of the "coloniality of power" that Mignolo talks about and that the history of folkloristics needs to be reconsidered with reference to colonialism.
2. More on types of folklore collections later in this chapter.
3. For a discussion on this "crisis in anthropology," see Diane Lewis, Anthropology and Colonialism, *Current Anthropology* 14, no. 5 (December 1973): 581–602.
4. Some of the most renowned colonial folklore collections are used by postcolonial independent states and their educational institutions as representative texts of their cultures. For example, Robert Sutherland Rattray and his African associate Malam Shahiu's collection of Hausa folklore remains the most important introduction to Hausa language and culture; Richard Carnac Temple's collections of the legends of Punjab were reprinted by Patiala University in Punjab and remain the best source on the subject; William Crooke and Pandit Chaube's collection of the folktales of northern India is unmatched by any postcolonial publication on the subject.
5. Diarmuid Ó Giolláin has discussed in detail the growth of folkloristics and its relationship to nationalism in Ireland in *Locating Irish Folklore* (2000). Pages 94–113

discuss the nineteenth-century Irish pioneers and show different political colors within Irish folklore collectors. Ó Giolláin analyzes folklore studies in Ireland in comparison with other European nations and nationalisms therein.
6. It is well known that British folklorists did not "theorize" and therefore did not articulate a colonial folklore theory. I contest this understanding, and will show in chapter 4 that theory was articulated and exists, albeit in fragments. From these fragments emerges a coherent whole with internal variations and contradictions.

CHAPTER 2. MOTIVE

1. Simla is a town in the Himalayas developed by the British as the summer retreat of British officers, their families, and even government offices.
2. Mary Frere's Indian ayah Anna Liberata de Souza narrated tales to her in English, and not in a local language. Frere wanted to record these tales because they entertained her very much, and she wanted to record them for her sister as well. A couple of serious reasons were only afterthoughts on her decision to record Anna's tales. Frere was aware that the tales could contribute to the discussions on folktales, but did not express that as a purpose of her record. She had expressed no scholarly reason and her individual situation did not engage with any philological or anthropological issues, yet her work gained immense popularity and scholarly attention in England (Narayan 2002). The reception clearly pointed to the presence of an interested public, print media, and scholars. Frere's success could itself become a motivating factor. It probably did, and similar collections (Stokes 1879; Steel and Temple 1884)—not guided by theoretical concerns and compiled from the narratives of domestic servants—appeared soon afterward.
3. Flora Anne Steel wanted to narrate for English nurseries and transport the English children into another world. Steel's motivation is expressed not in black and white but in the form of "Introductory," and she draws an unusual image—that of children as narrators. In Steel's enticing innocent tone the image is not without perspective. It compliments anthropological descriptions, here with regard to children, and in equally charming tone she puts another reason across: the timelessness of the tales she collected. Stories—now narrated for the children in the center of the Empire.
4. Georgiana Kingscote collected from her domestic servants, but her introduction to *Tales of the Sun* (1890) suggests that her main motive was to counter the propositions of the Benfey school regarding the status of Indian folktales, a subject we will discuss later. However, she expressed her motive in the last paragraph, as we have seen in the passage quoted earlier in chapter 2. It is a double-edged motive—to show the "peculiarities of Hindoos" and the "universal ... propensities" of storytelling. The motive is a very high aim; the tone is of the "ruler of the world," although the text is by a nonprofessional folklorist whose method does not bring her into the category of "scientific" folklore collectors, because it lacked the necessary analytical abstractions.
5. Alice Elizabeth Dracott published her first booklet in India without a preface or statement of her intentions. The quoted statement was written in her second collection, *Simla Village Tales, Or, Folk Tales from the Himalayas* (1906). There is no hint as to

what is meant by "Bookshelf of the World" and why is it written in uppercase. It seems England, or the western world of publishing, libraries, and readers, is meant. It may also be a metaphor for an artistic claim or goal—to make the tales part of international literary heritage.
6. Rev. Charles Swynnerton was academically inclined even though his "object" was "to amuse rather than to instruct." He expressed his awareness of folkloristic issues in his introduction to the tales, but intended his book to be a form of solace and pleasure to a variety of readers, romantically imagined by him. As in the quoted text, Rev. Swynnerton's easy manner also hides from our view how his privileges of power helped to resolve the problems of language he faced in the process of compiling his collection of stories. Swynnerton's easy manner was also reflected in the way he presented his materials and acknowledged his associates. There is no scientific classification attempted and no specific information on the tales or narrators given; "I have intentionally thrown my examples together almost haphazard," declares he. *Indian Nights' Entertainment, Folk Tales from Upper Indus, With Numerous Illustrations by Native Hands* is a beautifully illustrated volume and Swynnerton has only the following to say about the illustrators: "One word about the illustrations. They are the work of purely native draughtsmen" (xvi). Swynnerton's text included a discussion on Benfey's theory which we shall discuss later. For the present, this passage brings to the foreground that the market for collections of folktales from colonies, specifically India, was growing at a fast pace.
7. Rev. J. Hinton Knowles, the collector of folktales of Kashmir in India, admitted stages of motivation between collection and publication. In Knowles's statement the philological reasons led to folkloristic ones, and he ends with a particularly folkloristic motive—of preservation. Knowles's motives, strung together by needs and possibilities, led him to take some scientific measures in spite of not being a folklorist: He wrote notes to the stories and commented on variants (1888, ix). Knowles also explained Hindustani and Kashmiri words, and gave the name and address of the narrators in a glossary. His aim was not to amuse, but "to give them [tales] in a fair translation." Knowles's intentions had, however, not ended yet and he added, "I sincerely hope it will prove a real contribution towards that increasing stock of Folk-lore which is doing so much to clear away the clouds that envelop much of the practices, ideas and beliefs which make up the daily life of the natives of our great dependencies, control their feelings, and underlie many of their actions" (ix–x). Interestingly, the motives lay not just in personal needs and situations, but in the global context of colonial folkloristics. Knowles, like others, was aware that folklore from different colonies was reaching the center of the Empire, being taken cognizance of, and wished to be himself a part of it.
8. A simple and sympathetic-to-the-people missionary comes across through his words, and Gordon articulates a "threefold object"—the book was meant for "students of mankind," "officers of the Government" and "those who greatly desire to spread the religion of Christ in India" (vii). None of these "objects" were concerned with either the people among whom Gordon had lived, nor with the folktales he had heard and collected. Gordon's act of collection was part of his other role—that of a British missionary in a British colony who considers the work of the Empire and of Christ to be the same thing, and his folktales' collection is meant as service to those two great tasks.

9. With Richard Carnac Temple's *Legends of Punjab* (1883–1885), collection of Indian folklore became a scientific pursuit. Temple's work continues to remain the most important publication on the subject, and his writings are one of the clearest expressions of the paradigm of colonial folkloristics: exploitation of the tangible and intangible resources by the use of official power and machinery and the resultant folklore collection add a new shine to the collector's personality. Temple's motivation led him to engage with the theories being formulated back at home in the Folk-Lore Society, and to speak to the theorists at home from the colonial field, as it were. Temple gained a lot of fame from *Legends of Punjab*, was seen by the colonial state as a man knowledgeable about India, and was finally, in his retirement years, asked to speak on the importance of anthropology, wherein he titled his lecture appropriately as "On the Practical Value of Anthropology" (1904). More than two decades later, in 1928, he was appointed the president of the Jubilee Congress of the Folk-Lore Society.
10. The anthropological theme is clearly expressed in the statement of Augustus Mockler-Ferryman, a military officer, and finds an echo in the writings of many others—finding "survivals" of another stage of human history, of which the narratives are seen as important cultural elements. It is noteworthy how a hoary past is juxtaposed to an expected future. Ferryman-Mockler leaves it unspecified as to why the ideas of the "Negro" would have disappeared from practice, but the reference is crystal clear in the words of other collectors.
11. What Armitage called "civilization" was the colonial rule, which was indeed a major cause for all changes in the colonized societies, including changes in the situations of oral storytelling, social spaces and status of storytelling, value and meaning of narratives in real life, and the like. The colonial folklore collectors sensed that the folklore they were collecting was threatened by their own "civilization." This is a theme expressed also by folklorists and theorists at the center of the Empire. We will discuss the folklorists' position with regard to the changes in the chapter on interpretations. It is noteworthy here that, like their European counterparts in Europe, the colonial collectors too portrayed a "five-to-twelve" situation in many cases. The interesting difference is that here it was not the march of "modernity" which was threatening folklore—here the threat was from the system to which the collector himself belonged.
12. Mrs. A. B. Fisher (Ruth Fisher). The 1970 reprint volume of Ruth Fisher's *Twilight Tales of the Black Baganda* is introduced by Merrick Posnansky. He says, "Mrs. Fisher was the first foreigner in East Africa to write a book devoted mainly to the recitation and exegesis of oral history. To Roscoe, Johnston, and other writers of the period, history was incidental to their general description of the peoples in whom they were interested" (xii). In the same volume we learn that Ruth went to Uganda in 1900 to work for the Church Missionary Society, and in 1902 she married Rev. Arthur Bryan Fisher, who had been in Uganda since 1892, was well-known, and provided the major contacts for Ruth Fisher's work (xiii).
13. R. E. Dennett, the only trader who was a collector of folklore and writer of a number of works (1897, 1910, 1916) concerning anthropological and folkloristic matters. His experience of Africa was considerable and he felt that under the influence of the foreign rule and education, natives were now getting interested in their own culture. Dennett's

example shows the fissures in the cultural history and psychology of the colonized; a foreign education first takes them away from their "culture" and then they learn to look at it with the same intellectual paradigm of "culture" as their colonial masters and "look upon their native lore in a more serious light." The transition from one concept of "culture" and "history" to another is so fast that the changes can be tracked.

14. Smith and Dale decided to produce their book in 1909, but it did not appear until 1920. In between their decision and publication came many hurdles, the most important being World War I. Rev. Smith went to the front as a chaplain and Captain Dale was severely wounded in 1915, "invalided out of the army and returned to the British South Africa Company's service" (Smith and Dale 1920, x). They started again after the war, but just before the first printed pages of the book appeared Andrew Dale died of blackwater fever at Mumbwa, Northern Rhodesia (ibid., xv).

15. D. R. Mackenzie led an ethnographic survey in the Lake Nyasa region. The report produced and published has a separate section on folklore. Although the dramatis personae in this narrative of motivation are different, yet the contradiction is the same as in the above cases: that the "natives" themselves are aware that the white collector alone can save their lore. This time the collector has literally obliged the natives, upon the request of the "leading men of the tribe." This is a solitary example of its kind, where the collectors says that the "natives" wanted a record made.

16. R. Sutherland Rattray, one of the most important collectors of African folklore, found another special reason for his second work, on Hausa folklore: This observation, regarding Malamai, led Rattray to devise a novel method to document oral narratives—a case we will discuss in the next chapter, on methods. Rattray's case, however, shows that the reason to collect could be as completely impersonal as this: that the collector decided to collect because he found someone among the natives who could follow his system. Both illiteracy and literacy of the narrators could become the reason for the transformation of orality into writing. Rattray's life is a strange mix of perseverance and ambition. He attempted to learn many languages and intervene in the matters of governance on the basis of his knowledge of people's languages and folklore. He played an important role in the controversy regarding the golden stool of the Ashanti. Rattray is known to have had relationships with many African women and to have learned his languages from them. (Noel Machin, *Government Anthropologist: A Life of R. S. Rattray*, 1998.)

CHAPTER 3. METHOD

1. Regina Bendix in personal conversation, Göttingen, October 2004.
2. "Mirasi" means "hereditary professional" in Persian and Urdu.
3. This is a very common phrase with minor variations used by colonial collectors throughout the British Empire. With reference to India, see Naithani 2002b.
4. Smith and Dale 1920, page 334, has a photograph of an African man with headdress and bare shoulders, with the caption "A Mwila: A Great Teller of Tales."
5. See Naithani (2006a) for such a study of personal and intellectual engagement by a native associate.

6. "Belaitee" is a colloquial word for foreigner and in this case must have been the nickname for a traveling professional/seller. The description of the dress suggests that he may have come from Punjab, and may have been a Pathan from Afghanistan who went around the subcontinent selling dry fruits. "Oloo" means an owl and is used here as a nickname, probably given by fellow servants.
7. Onwumechili (2000) lecture IGBO ENWE EZE: *The Igbo Have No Kings* is about the way the Igbo people were forced to accept kings among their midst by the colonial rulers. The political structures of Igbo society functioned without a centralized authority like a king. In 1908 they were attacked by the British on the day of a festival, Akwo Abia. It is likely that this attack was led by Frank Hives, as suggested by Onwumechili. "The leaders of the British were identified as a certain *Ogba aji aka* (one with hairy arms) and a ruthless Major. In the 1950s, I read a book, *Juju and Justice in Nigeria*, by Frank Hives. He recorded that the natives called him *Agbajaka* because of his hairy arms. I therefore believe that Frank Hives was the man Inyi people called *Ogba aji aka*."
8. I have not been able to find this book, but Day talks about it in his introduction to his second book, *Folk Tales of Bengal* (1883).
9. *Wide Awake Stories* was first published in 1878. The comment on Day's *Folk Tales of Bengal* was added in the 1883 edition published after Day's work.

CHAPTER 4. THEORY

1. For a wide-ranging analysis of British colonial anthropology, its comparison with other European perspectives, and the postcolonial changes therein, see Sally Falk Moore, Changing Perspectives on a Changing Africa, in *Africa and the Disciplines*, ed. Robert H. Bates, V. Y. Mudimbe and Jean O'Barr (Chicago: University of Chicago Press, 1993), 3–97.
2. For an attempt to classify African folklore in terms of performers, see Dan Ben-Amos, Folklore in African Society, *Research in African Literatures* 6, no. 2 (Autumn 1975): 165–98.
3. I think Ralston is referring here to a very popular story: The Tale of Raja Harishchandra. The king was renowned as extremely truthful, honest, and charitable. His reputation made the gods jealous and one of them came to earth in the form of a mendicant to test the limits of Harishchandra's honesty, truthfulness, and kindness. In the course of the king's test events similar to those mentioned by Ralston take place.
4. Mary Kingsley's image reminds me of the witches with long brooms sweeping away winters to usher in the spring in Central European carnivals.
5. "Since the 1960s the study of colonialism has increasingly presented a view of colonialism as struggle and negotiation, analyzing how the dichotomous representations that Westerners use for colonial rule are the outcome of much more murky and complex practical interactions" (Pels 1997, 163).

CHAPTER 5. THE STORY-TIME OF THE BRITISH EMPIRE

1. The model of colonial folkloristics in the British Empire should be comparable to those in other colonial Empires, like the Spanish and the French, but an articulation of those models in the form of a study is not known to me.

REFERENCES

Allman, Jean, and John Parker. 2005. *Tongnaab: The History of a West African God.* Bloomington: Indiana University Press.

Anderson, Benedict. 1991. *Imagined Communities. Reflections on the Origin and Spread of Nationalism*, rev. ed. New York. Verso.

Balfour, Henry. 1923. The Welfare of Primitive Peoples. *Folk-Lore* 3–4 (1923): 12–24. Reprint, Wiesbaden: Kraus Reprint, 1969, 12–24.

Bascom, William. 1964. Folklore Research in Africa. *Journal of American Folklore* 77, no. 303 (January–March 1964): 12–31.

Bates, R. H., V. Y. Mudimbe, and J. O'Barr, eds. 1993. *Africa and the Disciplines. The Contribution of Research in Africa to the Social Sciences and Humanities.* Chicago: University of Chicago Press.

Bauman, Richard, and Charles Briggs. 2003. *Voices of Modernity. Language Ideologies and the Politics of Inequality.* Cambridge: Cambridge University Press.

Belsey, Catherine. 1980. *Critical Practice.* London: Methuen.

Ben-Amos, Dan: Folklore in Africa. *Research in African Literatures* 6, no. 2:165–98.

Bennett, Gillian. 1994. Geologists and Folklorists: Cultural Evolution and "The Science of Folklore." *Folklore* 105: 25–37

Blackburn, Stuart. 1996. *Inside the Drama House.* Berkeley: University of California Press.

———. 2003. *Print, Folklore and Nationalism in Colonial South India.* Delhi: Permanent Black.

Bonwick, James. 1870. *Daily Life and Origin of the Tasmanians.* London: Sampson Low.

Brabrook, E. W. 1901. H. M. Queen Victoria. *Folklore* 12: 98.

Browne, J. Orde. 1925. *The Vanishing Tribes of Kenya. A Description of the Manners and Customs of the Tribes Dwelling on the Vast Southern Slopes of Mount Kenya.* London: Seeley Service and Company.

Burne, Charlotte Sophia. 1914. *The Handbook of Folklore*, new ed., revised and enlarged. With an addendum (1957) by Sona Rosa Burnstein. London, Sidgwick and Jackson.

Cardinal, Allan Wolsey. 1920. *The Natives of the Northern Territories of the Gold Coast. Their Customs, Religions and Folklore.* London: George Routledge and Sons.

Canclini, Nestor Garcia. 1995. *Hybrid Cultures. Strategies for Entering and Leaving Modernity*. Minneapolis: University of Minnesota Press.

Chakraborty, Dipesh. 2000. *Provincializing Europe: Postcolonial Thought and Historical Difference*. New Jersey: Princeton University Press.

Crooke, William. 1892. *Popular Religion and Folklore of Northern India*. Allahabad: Government Press.

———. 1912. The Scientific Aspects of Folklore. *Folk-Lore* 23:14–32.

Crooke, William, and Pandit Ram Gharib Chaube. 2002. *Folktales from Northern India*. Santa Barbara, Calif.: ABC-CLIO.

Day, Lal Behari, Rev. 1912 (1883). *Folk Tales of Bengal. With 32 Illustrations in Colour by Warwick Goble*. London: Macmillan.

Dennett, R. E. 1897. *Notes on the Folklore of Fjort, French Congo*. Introduction by Mary Kingsley. Published by FOLK-LORE Society. London: David Nutt. Reprint, Nendeln/Lichtenstein: Kraus Reprint Limited, 1967.

———. 1910. *Nigerian Studies. The Religious and Political System of the Yoruba*. London: Macmillan.

———. 1911. *Notes on West African Categories*. London: Macmillan.

———. 1916. *The Ogboni and Other Secret Societies in Nigeria*. Reprinted from the Journal of the African Society. FLS [Pamph.] C67 Nig DEN.

Doke, Clement Martyn. 1927. *Lamba Folklore*. New York: AFS Publication.

Dorson, Richard M. 1968. *The British Folklorists*. Chicago: University of Chicago Press.

Dracott, Alice. 1896. *Folktales from Central India*. Allahabad: Pioneer Press.

———. 1906. *Simla Village Tales*. London: John Murray.

Driberg, J. H. 1923. *The Lango, a Nilotic Tribe of Uganda*. London: Unwin.

Elkin, A. P. 1938. *The Australian Aborigines. How to Understand Them*. Sydney: Argus and Robertson.

Ellis, Alfred Burdon. 1890. *The Ewe Speaking People of the Slave Coast of West Africa, Their Religion, Manner, Custom, Laws, Language*. London: Chapman and Hall.

Fisher, Ruth. 1911. *Twilight Tales of the Baganda*. London: Marshall Brothers. Reprint, with a new introduction by Merrick Posnansky, London: Cass, 1970.

Fletcher, Roland S. 1912.. *Hausa Sayings and Folklore, With a Vocabulary of New Words*. London: Oxford University Press.

Foucault, Michelle. 1972. *The Archaeology of Knowledge*. London: Routledge.

Frazer, James G. 1890. *The Golden Bough*. London: Macmillan. Reprint, Touchstone, 1995.

Frere, Mary. 1868. *Old Deccan Days*. Reprint, London: John Murray, 1929.

Furniss, Graham, and Liz Gunner, eds. 1995. *Power, Marginality and African Oral Literature*. Cambridge: Cambridge University Press.

Furniss, Graham, and Philip J. Jagger, eds. 1988. *Studies in Hausa Language and Linguistics*. London: Kegan Paul.

Gordon, E. M. 1909. *Indian Folk Tales: Being Side-Lights on Village Life in Bilaspore, Central Provinces*. London, Elliot Stock.

Grierson, George Abraham, ed. 1985. *Linguistic Survey of India (1894–1927)*. Delhi: Cosmo Publications.

Gyekye, Kwame. 1988. *The Unexamined Life: Philosophy and the African Experience*. Accra: Ghana Universities Press.
Hartland, E. Sidney. 1901. Presidential Address, 1900. *Folklore* 9, no. 1 (March 1901): 14–15.
Herder, Johann Gottfried. 1846. *Stimmen der Völker in Liedern (1778–1779). Gesammelt, geordnet, zum Teil übersetzt*. Stuttgart und Tübingen: Gottascher Verlag.
Hives, Frank, and Gascoigne Lumley. 1930. *Ju-Ju and Justice in Nigeria*. London: John Lane.
Hobsbawm, Eric, and Terrence Ranger, eds. 1983. *The Invention of Tradition*. Cambridge: Press Syndicate of the University of Cambridge.
Honko, Lauri. 1996. Epic and Identity: National, Regional, Communal, Individual. *Oral Tradition* 11, no. 1 (1996): 18–36. http://journal.oraltradition.org/issues/11i/honko.
Jason, Heda. 1983. India on the Map of "Hard Science" Folkloristics. *Folklore* 94:105–7.
Kingscote, Georgiana, and Pandit Natesa Sastri. 1890. *Tales of the Sun; or, Folklore of Southern India*. London: W. H. Allen.
Kingsley, Mary. 1897. *Travels in West Africa*. London: Macmillan.
Kiwanuka, M. S. M. 1968. Bunyoro and the British: A Reappraisal of the Causes for the Decline and Fall of an African Kingdom. *Journal of African History* 9, no. 4:603–19.
Knowles, J. Hinton. 1888. *Folk Tales of Kashmir*. London: Trübner.
Koelle, Sigismund Wilhelm. 1854. *African Native Literatures, or Proverbs, Tales, Fables, and Historical Fragments in the Kanuri or Borno Language*. London.
Lang, Andrew. 1887. *Myth, Ritual and Religion*. Reprint from 1913 ed., London: Senate, 1995.
———. 1901. *Magic and Religion*. London: Longmans, Green and Company.
Lassiter, James E. 1999. African Culture and Personality: Bad Social Science, Effective Social Activism, or a Call to Reinvent Ethnology? *African Studies Quarterly* 3, no. 2: 1, available at http://web.africa.ufl.edu/asq/v3/v3i3a1.htm.
Lewin, T. H. 1870. *Wild Races of South-Eastern India*. London: W. H. Allen.
Machin, Noel. 1998. *Government Anthropologist: A Life of R. S. Rattray*. Canterbury: Centre for Social Anthropology and Computing Monographs.
Mackenzie, C. F. 1882. *The Romantic Land of Hind*. London. Allen.
Mackenzie, D. R. 1925. *The Spirit-Ridden Konde. A Record of the Customs and Ideas Gathered Amongst Inhabitants of the Lake Nyasa Region*. London: Seeley Service and Company.
Mbiti, John S. 1969. *African Religions and Philosophy*. New York: Praeger Publishers.
Mignolo, Walter D. 2000. *Local Histories/Global Designs: Coloniality, Sub-Altern Knowledges, and Border Thinking*. New Jersey: Princeton University Press.
Mills, Margaret. 2009. Personal communication, Ohio State University, March 2009.
Mockler-Ferryman, Major Augustus F. 1900. *West Africa: Its Rise and Progress*. London: Swan Sonnenschein.
Mudimbe, V. Y. 1988. *The Invention of Africa*. Bloomington: Indiana University Press.
———. 1991. *Parables and Fables, Exegesis, Textuality and Politics in Central Africa*. Madison: University of Wisconsin Press.
Naithani, Sadhana, ed. 2002a. *Folktales from Northern India: William Crooke and Pandit Ram Gharib Chaube*. Santa Barbara, Calif.: ABC-CLIO, 2002. Indian Edition: Delhi, Shubhi Publications, 2005.

———. 2002b. "Prefaced Space." In *Imagined States: Nationalism, Utopia and Longing in Oral Cultures*, ed. Luisa Del Giudice and Gerald Porter. Logan: Utah State University Press.

———. 2002c. "To Tell a Tale Untold." *Journal of Folklore Research* 2–3:201–16.

———. 2006a. *In Quest of Indian Folktales*. Bloomington: Indiana University Press.

———. 2006b. Of Ghosts and Colonizers. In *Sites of Resistance—Textual Tactics*, ed. Madhu Benoit, Susanne Berthier-Foglar, and Linda Carter. Editions Le Manuscrit. 2006.

Narayan, Kirin, ed. 2002. *Old Deccan Days*, by Mary Frere (1868). Santa Barbara, Calif.: ABC-CLIO.

Ntara, Samuel Yosia. 1934. *Man of Africa*. Translated and arranged from the original Nyanja by T. Cullen Young. Foreword by Professor Julian Huxley. London: The Religious Tract Society.

Nyasani, J. M. 1997. *The African Psyche*. Nairobi: University of Nairobi and Theological Printing Press.

Oakley, F. Sherman. 1905. *Holy Himalaya (Kumaon and Garhwal)*. Edinburgh: Oliphant, Anderson and Ferrier.

Ó Giolláin, Diarmuid. 2000. *Locating Irish Folklore: Tradition, Modernity, Identity*. Cork: Cork University Press.

Onwumechili, Cyril Agodi. 2000. *Igbo Enwe Eze: The Igbo Have No Kings*. http://ahiajoku.igbonet.com/2000/.

Parker, K. Langloh. 1898. *More Australian Legendary Tales*. Collected from various tribes, with introduction by Andrew Lang. London: Nutt.

———. 1905. *The Euahlayi Tribe. A Study of Aboriginal Life in Australia*. With an introduction by Andrew Lang. London: Constable.

Pels, Peter. 1997. The Anthropology of Colonialism: Culture, History and the Emergence of Governmentality. *Annual Review of Anthropology* 26:163–83.

Pratt, Mary Louise. 1992. *Imperial Eyes: Travel Writing and Transculturation*. London: Routledge.

Rattray, Robert Sutherland. 1907. *Some Folk-Lore Stories as Songs in Chinyanja*, with English translations and notes. London: Oxford University Press.

———. 1913. *Hausa Folk-Lore*. Oxford, Clarendon.

———. 1923. *Ashanti* (illustrated). Oxford: Oxford University Press.

Ray, Benjamin. 1984. James G. Frazer's Correspondence with John Roscoe, 1907–1924. *History in Africa* 11:397

Roscoe, John. 1911. *The Baganda: An Account of their Native Customs and Beliefs*. London: Macmillan.

———. 1923. *The Bakitara or Banyoro*. Cambridge: Cambridge University Press.

Rouse, W. H. D. 1899. *The Talking Thrush and Other Tales from India*. Collected by William Crooke and retold by W. H. D. Rouse. London. J. M. Dent.

Rowe, John A. 1967. Review of *The Baganda. An Account of their Native Customs and Beliefs*, by the Rev. John Roscoe, 2nd ed. (London: Cass, 1965). *Journal of African History* 8, no. 1:163–66.

Smith, Edwin, and Andrew Dale. 1920. *The Ila-Speaking People of Northern Rhodesia*. London: Macmillan.

Steel, Flora Anne, and Richard Carnac Temple. 1884. *Wide Awake Stories*. London: Trübner and Company.

Stokes, Maive. 1879. *Indian Fairy Tales*. ["One Hundred Copies Privately Printed in Calcutte."] London: Ellis and White.

Swynnerton, Rev. Charles. 1892. *Indian Nights Entertainment. Folk Tales from Upper Indus. With Numerous Illustrations by Native Hands*. London: Elliot Stock.

Taplin, Rev. G. 1879. *The Folklore, Manners, Customs and Languages of the South Australian Aborigines*. Gathered from Inquiries made by authority of South Australian Government. Adelaide. E. Spiller, Acting Government Printer.

Talbot, Percy Amaury. 1923. *Life in Southern Nigeria. The Magic, Beliefs and Customs of the Ibibio Tribe*. London: Macmillan.

Temple, Richard Carnac. 1904 "On the Practical Value of Anthropology." Sir R. C. Temple, Miscellaneous Papers. British Library.

———. 1930. The Mind and Mental Atmosphere. *Folk-Lore*.

———. 1962. *Legends of Punjab*, vol. 1–3 (1883–1885). Patiala: Punjabi University Press.

Torrend, J. 1921. *Specimens of Bantu Folk-Lore from Northern Rhodesia. Texts (collected with the help of the Phonograph) and English Translations. With musical illustrations*. London. Kegan Paul, Trench, Trübner and Company.

Weeks, John H. 1911. *Congo Life and Folklore*. London: The Religious Tract Society.

White, Luise, Stephen Miescher, and David William Cohen, eds. 2002. *African Words, African Voices: Critical Practices in Oral History*. Bloomington: Indiana University Press.

Index

Aboya, Victor, 45, 68, 69
Africa, 12–13; Chinyanja people in, 31; colonial collectors from, 81, 82, 85; concepts of individual and self, 117–18; culture of, 35, 100; in English, 13; folklore of, 3, 4, 26, 101, 119; Hausa people in, 31; history of, 122; motives in, 16–18; mythological narratives of, 123; narratives of, 90, 96; problem of unwritten languages in, 35; tales, 110; theory in folklore collection, 109–11; translation of, 31–32; tribal societies of, 42; tribes, study of, 101; by "Western" scholars, 127. *See also* West Africa
African scholars, 125
"agricultural terminology," collection of, 73
Allman, Jean, 68, 69
"Amazing Methods," 27, 43, 51–64
American folklorists, 124
ancestor-worship, 81
Andaman and Nicobar Islands, 12
Anderson, Benedict, 5, 129n1
"animal tales," 94, 95
anthropology, 3; colonial, criticism of, 3; enquiries, 9; theories, folklore studies and, 106
Armitage, C. H., 16, 132n11
Arnason, *Icelandic Stories*, 65
Arofa odes/poems, 39
Ashanti people, Nigeria: controversy among, 20; study of, 45, 46
Asia, culture: folklore collection of, 4; study of, 100

Australia: aborigines in, 62, 63; "amazing" method in, 61; folklore of, 4, 6, 26; methods of colonial collectors in, 52

Baganda, The, 12–13, 78
Ba-ila, history of, 92–93
Bakitara tribe. *See* Banyoro tribe
Balfour, Henry, 6, 62, 125, 126
"ballad," 116
Bantu dialect, 38
Bantu tribe, 38, 92; folklore of, 86, 122; tales of, 83
Banyoro tribe, in Africa, 34
bards, roaming, in Punjab, 29–30
Barlow, Thomas Lambert, 80
Bascom, William, 3
Bates, Robert H., 134n1
Bauman, Richard, 129n1, 123
beliefs: of barbaric tribes, 107; in narratives, 60; traditional, 8, 9, 16, 37, 46
Belsey, Catherine, 76
Ben-Amos, Dan, 134n2
Benedix, Regina, 24, 133n16
Benfey, Theodor, 98, 100, 101, 102, 105
Bengali folktales, 65
Benjamin, 58, 59, 60
Bennett, Gillian, 102, 110
black magic, 42
Blackburn, Stuart, 35, 36, 70
Bleek, Wilhelm Heinrich Immanuel, 13, 62
Bonwick, James, 61, 63
Brabrook, E. W., 19
Briggs, Charles, 123, 129n1

British anthropologists, 101
British colonialism, and cultural network, 7
British colonies, folklore of, 4
British Empire, 2; folklorist activity in, 12; linguistic policy of, 25; method of folklore collection in, 72; story-time of, 115; theory and folklore of, 100–11
British folklore collectors, 3, 25, 100; and native folk narrators, 70
British folklore studies, 3
British Folklorists, The, 26, 27
Browne, Cranville, 70, 71, 110
Bunyoro, king of, 40
Burial Secret Societies, account of, 39
Burma, 12, 104, 105
Burne, Charlotte, 8, 21, 22, 76; *Handbook of Folk-Lore*, 73

Callaway, Cannon, 13
calligraphy, 67
Campbell, 65
Canclini, Garcia, 127; theory of "hybridity" of, 125
Cardinall, A. W., 16, 17
Chakraborty, Dipesh, 123; *Provincializing Europe*, 50
Chaube, Ram Gharib, 45, 50, 51, 74, 75, 81, 109, 119, 129n4
Chinyanja folklores, 45, 67, 103
Christian missions, 35
Christianity, 53, 60; influence over Fjort in West Africa, 99–100
cinema, 6, 32
Clouston, W. A., 102
colonial anthropology, critique of, 103
colonial archives, native folklorists of, 64–72
colonial culture theory, 114
colonial folklore/folklorists: collections, 9–10, 43; collectors, 3, 10, 23, 36, 50, 65; context of, 11; as global, 115–16, 119, 128; politics of, 121–28; relationship with state, 121; scholarship, 4, 7, 73, 74, 111; social relationship with narrators, 55; theory, 112. *See also* British folklore

colonial folkloristic method, 44, 51
colonial hegemony, 2
colonial officials, compilation of folklore by, 45
colonialism, 1, 3, 7, 36, 56, 64, 75, 100, 124, 134n5; anthropological view of, 94; and cultural disjunction, 128; and cultural network, 7; ideology of, 113; and influence on folklore, 61; theory and culture politics of, 4
"colonized," silence of, 46
Congo, 52–53
Cosquin, M. Emanuel, 102
Crooke, William, 9, 20, 42, 45, 50, 51, 61, 70, 72, 73, 74, 75, 98, 106, 107, 108, 111, 118, 119, 121, 122, 129n4
cross-cultural perception, 2
culture: context and confrontation, 61; definition of, 4, 98; disjunctions, theory of, 115; identity, 124; otherness of colonial collectors, 47, 76
customs and beliefs: traditional, 8; writings on, 9

Dale, Andrew, 13, 17, 24, 31, 32, 37, 39, 70, 71, 84, 92–95, 110, 133n14, 134n8; *The Ila Speaking People of Northern Rhodesia*, 87, 90–91; *Wide Awake Stories*, 71; writing on performances, 38
dance, 6
Day, Rev. Lal Behari, 65–66; *Folk-Tales of Bengal*, 65; *Peasant Life in Bengal*, 65
de Souza, Anna Liberata, 29, 55

Dennett, R. E., 13, 17, 39, 72, 82, 87, 89, 96, 132n13
developing societies, cultural notions and ideological perceptions in, 2
"Dinapur Wala Sahib," "short-story" of, 60
Doke, Clement, 38, 39, 72, 89, 115; collection of Lamba folktales, 86, 96
Dorson, Richard M., 9, 11, 21, 26, 43, 49, 76, 78, 102

Dracott, Alice Elizabeth, 15, 54–56, 130n5; *Folktales from Central India*, 54
Driberg, J. H., 36

East India Company, 21
education, influence on culture, 40
Elkin, A. P., 63
"empire," identity of, 5
empirical theory, 79–85
empiricism, role in colonial folkloristics, 79
England, folklore collection in, 12
English education, spread of, 21
English language texts, 7
ethical transgression, 44
Eurocentrism, 73
Europe, naturalists within, 18
European concept, of folklore, 48
European folklore, 32, 73, 102, 112, 120; collection, 1; scholarship, 65

"festival of ceremonies," 40
Fisher, A. B. (Ruth), 17, 69, 71, 132n12
Fjort, of West Africa, 99; collection and classification of, 87, 89; narration among, 82
Fletcher, Rolands, 17
folklore collection, 1, 3, 25; compilation of, 8, 23–24; and cultural identity, 76; and "folklife," 95; genres, 116; history of, 1; interpretation from, 89–100; narratives of experience of collectors, 36, 37; performers, 84–85; research on, 1, 10, 40, 47–48; scholarship, 23, 101, 115, 121–22, 127; socio-political implications of, 1; studies, 2
folklore collectors, 1, 34; discourses of, 21; experience of, 36, 37; male missionaries, 9, 10; officials, 9, 10; types of, 9–10; women, 9, 10. *See also* British folklore collectors
folklore educational institutions, in U.S., 119
Folk-Lore Society, London, 3, 4, 6, 19, 36, 62, 72, 74, 78, 100, 101, 102, 106, 110

folkloristics: development of, 48; methods, 10, 11, 28–43, 75; motives, 10, 13, 14–20, 22; post-colonial perspectives, 43–51; as scholars, 112; science of, 10; theory, 10
Foucault, Michel, 2, 123
Frazer, James G., 33, 78, 100, 101, 104, 107, 109; *The Golden Bough*, 102
Frere, Mary, 13, 14, 28, 29, 49, 55, 81, 96, 97, 98, 121, 130n2
Furniss, Graham, 118, 124

German philologists, 101
Germany, 19; romantic naturalist movement in study, 100
"ghost stories," 60–61
Gilchrist, *Pleasant Stories*, 21
Gordon, E. M., 15–16, 131n8
Great Britain, as locale for folklore collection, 5. *See also* England
Greece, 81, 82
Grierson, George Abraham, 116
Grimm, Jacob and Wilhelm, 1, 26, 44, 45, 65, 76, 77, 79, 85, 100, 127; *Children's and Household Tales*, 77
Gunner, Liz, 124
Gyekye, Kwame, 117

haiku poems, 28, 42
Handbook of Folklore, 22
Hartland, E. Sidney, 19
Hausa folklore, 12, 45, 103, 129n4, 133n16
Hausa society, 67
Herder, J. G., 76, 79
Highland Stories, 65
Hindoo folklore, 14
historiography, of colonial collectors, 44
Hives, Frank, 52; narratives of, 56–60; "The Rest House," 57
Hobsbawm, Eric, 123
Huxley, Julian, 66

Icisimikisyo, 86
identity building, 5

Ifa, 39
"Il Musannif." *See* Mackenzie, C. F.
Ila-speaking people, Northern Rhodesia, narratives of, 31, 32, 84, 87
"Imagined Community," 5
"Imperial Gaze, The," 2
India: authenticity to folklore from, 29; folklore collection from, 13, 26, 81, 85; folktales from, 88, 96–99, 101; motives in, 13–16; South, history of printing folklore in, 35; tales from South, 97; "western" scholars on folklore, 127
Ireland, 7
Islamic narrative traditions, influence of, 29

Jagger, Philip J., 124
Jason, Heda, 9, 21
Jatakas, 105
Johnson, Bishop, 39
ju-ju worship, in narratives, 58, 59, 60

Kagwa, Apolo, 12, 41, 109
Kashmir: as field of folklore literature, 15, 79; folktales from, 105, 131n7
Kingscote, Georgiana, 14, 81, 97, 130n4
Kingsley, Mary, 13, 74, 84, 87, 89, 95, 96, 99–100, 121, 134n4
Kiwanuk, M. S. M., 109
Knowles, J. Hinton, 15, 79, 81, 105–6, 131n7
Koelle, Wilhelm, 13
Konde, in Africa, 18

Lamba people, folktales of, 38, 86, 95
Lang, Andrew, 100, 101, 102, 104, 109
language, problem of, 26
Lassiter, James, 124, 125
"legal stories," 95–96
Legend of Punjab, 29
Lepsius, standard alphabet of, 35
Lewin, T. H., 20
Lewis, Diane, 129n3
Liberata, Anna, narration of Hindu society, 66

Lijadu, Rev., 39
linguistic policy, of British Empire, 25
linguistic politics, 116
listening, culture of, 38
"literal translation," 36
Lonrott, Elias, 64
Lumley, Gascoigne, 56–57, 58

Mackenzie, C. F., 52
Mackenzie, D. R., 18, 133n15
Mackie Ethnological Report, on tribes of Central Africa, 33
Mahabharata, 105
Manjhi, Akbar Shah, 81, 84
Märchen, 85
Marrett, Prof., 30, 67, 68, 103
Mbiti, John S., 117
medicine men, 41
Mignolo, Walter, 23, 73, 113, 129n1
Mills, Margaret, 105
mirasis (professional singers), 29
missionaries: compilation of folklore by, 45; education by, 39
Mockler-Ferryman, Augustus, 16
modernity: process in colonies, 40; tradition and colonial folkloristics, 122–28
"Momia Wala Sahib," "ghost story" of, 60
Moore, Sally Falk, 134n1
Mudimbe, V. Y., 8, 113, 123, 134n1
Mukuni tale, 83
Mull, Chaina, 45, 49, 88
Muller, Max, 100, 101, 105; solar theory of, 102; study of Vedas, 107
museums, 6
mythological narratives, 105, 123

Naga tribes, 62
Naithani, Sadhana, 61, 74, 129n1, 133n5
Nankani social life, treatise on, 68
Narayan, Kirin, 139n2
narratives: interpretation of, 113; as pleasure of life, 38; songs in northern India, 116

narrators: of folktales, 29, 30, 31, 38, 40, 55, 70; status of, 120; stigmatization of, 42
nation, "imagined," 5
"national Hindoo characteristics," reflection in tales, 97
"nationalism," 7
nationalist movement, 18–19
"nationalist" scholarship, of folklore in colonies, 4
native collectors: as assistants to colonial collectors, 48–50, 70; of folklore, 10, 38–39, 42; knowledge about, 5
"Native" Folklorists of Colonial Archives, 27
"native" languages, transformation from, 8
Nigeria, 17
Nigerian Chronicle, 39
Norse tales, 65
north Indian folktales, 5
Northern Rhodesia: collection of folktales from, 37; Ila-speaking people of, 87
Ntara, Samuel Yosia, 66–67, 75; *Man in Africa*, 66
Nyasani, J. M., 125
Nzambi stories, 87

Oakley, E. Sherman, 82
O'Barr, Jean, 134n1
Ó Giolláin, Diarmuid, 1, 7, 129–30n5
Old Deccan Days, 13, 29
Onwumechili, 134n7
oral culture: aspects of, 38; in colonies, 5–6; expressive, 7
oral discourse, 3
oral folklore, 28–37, 121; classification of texts of, 85–89; limitations of, 32
oral narratives, 1
orality, 5–6, 8, 83; recording of, 24, 27; and writing, 71, 118
"Orientalism," 2, 7, 39, 46
orthography, problem of, in Africa and South Asia, 35

Panchatantra, 102
paper, scarcity of, 35–36

Parker, K. Langloh, 63–64, 68, 69; *More Australian Legends*, 62
Pels, Peter, 46, 94, 134n5
"performance": and observance of folklore, 37–43; theory, 37
"periphery," 5
Persian narrative traditions, influence of, 29
Phillips, Bishop, 39
philosophical studies, 110
photography, 6
poetic expression, 2, 123
"popular antiquities," collection of, 73
Posnansky, Merrick, 132n12
"post-colonial theory," 1, 2
"post-modernity," 127
Power, Marginality and African Oral Literature, 124
Pratt, Mary Louise, 2
"primitive" people: study of, 100; use of the term, 118
printing presses, scarcity of, 35
psychology, folklore and, 108
Punjab, 12; folklore from, 79–80, 88, 106; roaming bards in, 29

Ralston, 98, 106, 134n3
Ranger, Terrence, 123
Rasalu, as solar myth, 106
Rattray, Robert Sutherland, 12, 13, 18, 20, 30, 31, 32, 47, 67–69, 103, 119, 121, 124, 129n4, 133n16; *Hausa Folk-Lore*, 67; study on Ashanti people, 45, 46; *The Tribes of the Asante Hinterland*, 68
Revolt of 1857, India, 123
Rome, glory of, 81, 82
Roscoe, John, 12, 13, 33–34, 40, 78, 109, 132n12; *The Baganda*, 41, 42; method of research, 34–35
Rouse, W. H. D., 9
Rowe, John, 13, 41, 42, 78

Said, Edwards, 2, 7; concept of "Orientalism," 46
Sastri, Pandit Natesa, and of Folk-Lore Society, 70

"scientific" nature, of folklore collection, 9, 28, 36, 37, 72
Scotland, 7
Shaihu, Malam, dictating oral text by, 71, 119, 124, 129n4
Simla, 12
Smith, Edwin, 13, 17, 24, 31, 32, 37–39, 84, 92–95, 110, 133n4; classification of Ila-speaking people, 87; *The Ila-Speaking People of Northern Rhodesia*, 90–91, 117
society, knowledge about, 2
socio-political contexts, 115, 117
songs, traditional, 8
South Asia: scholars in, 124; study of folklore in, 6; written tradition and orthography in, 35
speaking, and writing, problem of speed between, 36
Steel, Flora Anna, 13, 14, 130n2–3; *Wide Awake Stories*, 71
Stokes, Maive, 13, 81, 98, 130n2
stories: collection, reasons for, 21; -telling, 14, 37, 60, 120, 128; traditional, 8, 68
Studies in Hausa Language and Linguistics, 124
Sulwe, tales of, in Africa, 87
Sulwe and Fulwe, folktales of, 90–91
superstitions, 42
Swyannerton, Rev. Charles, 13, 15, 42, 79–81, 88, 97, 105, 128, 131n6

Talbot, Percy Carnac, 81
Tamil language, in print, 35
Taplin, Rev., 61–62
Tasmania, 6
Tasmanians, extermination of, 62
technology, problem of, 35, 36
Temple, Richard Carnac, 12, 13, 14, 16, 20, 29, 31, 32, 33, 42, 45, 49, 65, 66, 70, 71, 72, 80, 88, 98, 103–6, 108, 121, 129n4, 130n2, 132n9; translations of bards by, 30
"theory," in folkloristics, 76
Thomas, William John, 21, 73
Tonga storytellers, 83

Torrend, J., 35, 83; on Bantu folklore, 122
tradition, modernity and colonial folkloristics, 122–28
translations, of folklores, 31–34, 36, 44, 51
transnational folklorists, development of, 119

United Kingdom, 4; relationship with colonies, 6. *See also* England
United States, 3, 119

Wales, 7
Weeks, John, 13, 52–54; *Congo Life and Folklore*, 52
West Africa, 18; folklore of, 16
westernization, in colonies, 40
women, as storytellers in colonies, 70–71
World War I, 77
World War II, 77

Young, T. Cullen, 66
Yoruba Death, account of, 39

www.ingramcontent.com/pod-product-compliance
Lightning Source LLC
Chambersburg PA
CBHW030345240426
43661CB00052B/1747